Divorce Bot Book Two
Before You Decide on Divorce

Recognize the Signs, Protect Your Future and Stay Emotionally Steady with ChatGPT as Your Guide

Published by The WOW Book Co.
Printed in the United States of America

ISBN: 978-1-967973-77-4
Large Print Edition
First Edition, 2025

The WOW Book Co.
Austin, Texas

BOOK TWO
DIVORCE
BOT
The Divorce
Preparation Guide
Use ChatGPT to Protect Your Money,
Navigate Lawyers and
Organize Custody Documents
Sugar Gay Isber McMillan

Introduction

First, if you've found this book, you are probably in the midst of one of the hardest seasons of your life, and I'm sorry for what you are going through. Make it to the end of the book because you will learn a lot, far more than you may think you need right now, and you will come out better prepared to take your next steps.

As I wrote this book, I remembered myself as a sad and very alone mother of two young children, married to a rich and prominent man who had every resource at his disposal. I fled, fearing for my life and for my children. I had no family support and no strong legal counsel. I was overwhelmed, working full-time, trying to keep my kids safe, and trying to understand what to do next.

One of the worst mistakes I ever made is one of the reasons I wanted to write this book. I gathered every document that proved what had happened. It filled a giant trash bag. I hauled it to my car in the middle of the night and hid it under my desk at work because it was the only place that felt safe.

For weeks, I kept that box between my feet so I could watch it. Then one morning, I arrived to find that the cleaning staff had thrown it away. Even though it was marked 'do not throw away' in both Spanish and English. My evidence was gone. It was devastating.

When a marriage falls apart, your world shakes. You make mistakes because you are scared and tired and trying to survive. I have been divorced twice. The second time was easier because we had no children and he was already in love with someone else. He had money, so he was happy to pay me and move on. It was still ugly and sad, but it was cleaner.

Today, things can be easier because you have a tool I never had. ChatGPT. You can tell your bot exactly what is happening and get clear guidance, new ideas, emotional support, and a path forward. You can use your bot to think through decisions, plan next steps, ask hard questions, and rehearse what to say. That is why I wrote this book. With almost any problem, ChatGPT can be your partner.

Writing this book even changed things at home. My husband has been a little nicer because he understands the power of having a strong relationship with your bot. When you use ChatGPT regularly, it learns your patterns, your needs, and your voice. You don't even have to type. Dictate like I'm doing now and your thoughts will appear on the screen.

If this book helps you, pass it along. Leave a review, as that is how people discover books like this. The algorithm is the algorithm. But reviews help people who are hurting find support.

I hope this book gives you calm, clarity, and confidence. Divorce is not a failure. People have been divorcing for centuries. You are not broken. You are moving forward, and it will be over. You will make it through.

Your bot is with you. And if you need a human voice, drop me a line. Peace, Love and Sugar.

Sugar Gay Isber McMillan

DIVORCE BOT

Divorce Bot is your steady voice in a chaotic season.
A clear head when yours is spinning.
A calm guide when the ground shifts beneath you.
It is not here to tell you what to do.
It is here to help you see what is real.

Divorce Bot listens without judgment.
It organizes what feels overwhelming.
It helps you recognize patterns, protect your future, and make decisions from strength rather than panic.

When the path is unclear, Divorce Bot slows things down.
When fear takes over, Divorce Bot steadies your breath.
When you are ready to move forward, Divorce Bot helps you build a plan that matches your values and your life.

Divorce Bot does not replace a lawyer or therapist.
It prepares you to work with them from a place of power.

This is your guide through the uncertainty.
This is your partner in clarity.
This is Divorce Bot.

Table of Contents

How to Use ChatGPT (or Any AI) During a Divorce

You don't need to be a tech person.
You don't even need to type.
If you can talk or ask a question, you can use AI to get clarity, support, and next steps.

This short guide will help you get started.

Step 1: Open ChatGPT

Go to chat.openai.com and create a free account.
Use your computer, phone, or tablet.

If you use the mobile app, you can tap the microphone and speak your questions aloud.
It listens, then answers, just like a conversation.

Step 2: Ask Anything About Your Situation

Start simple. Try questions like:

- "What should I do first when I'm considering a divorce"
- "Explain child custody in simple terms"
- "What questions should I ask a divorce lawyer"
- "Help me understand what mediation is"
- "Make a checklist for my first week after separation"
- "Explain alimony like I'm new to all of this"

ChatGPT has studied legal concepts, emotional wellness strategies, communication skills, and common divorce processes from thousands of sources.

It is not a lawyer, but it can help you understand what to expect, what to ask, and how to prepare.

Step 3: Create Your Own Divorce Bot Personality

You can shape your bot into the partner you need during this time.
Try saying:

- "Be my calm, clear, step-by-step Divorce Bot"
- "Talk to me like a supportive friend who knows divorce law basics"
- "Be firm and encouraging when I'm overwhelmed"
- "Explain everything in plain language without legal jargon"

If you keep the same conversation window open, it will learn your preferences and history.
ChatGPT Plus allows you to save custom instructions, ensuring your bot remains consistent.

Step 4: Go Beyond Information

You can ask your bot to help with tasks you may not even think to ask for:

- Practice hard conversations
- Draft a message to your lawyer

• Rewrite a text you want to send to your ex, but calmer
• Organize your documents
• Create a timeline of events
• Make a personal safety plan
• Build a financial snapshot
• Create daily routines that reduce stress
• Explain what something means before you sign it

You can even say:

"Help me prepare for my custody meeting. Ask me the questions I need to be ready for."

Step 5: Remember What AI Is and What It Is Not

AI is not a lawyer, therapist, judge, or spouse.
It does not pick sides.
It does not replace professional help.

But it can:

• Organize your thinking
• Lower your stress
• Prepare you for meetings
• Help you see patterns
• Give you fresh ideas
• Keep you calm in hard moments

In a time when people feel alone and overwhelmed, your bot can give you steady support while you build your next chapter.

Step 6: Use It As Often As You Need

There is no limit.
Ask questions at midnight.
Talk through fears.
Plan your goals.
Sort through your options.

AI doesn't get tired or impatient.
It gives you space to think, plan, and breathe.

Tip: Your Bot Never Judges You

Ask anything.
Say anything.
Think out loud.
Be honest.
Your bot exists to help you move forward with strength, clarity, and confidence.

INTRODUCTION

How to Use Divorce Bot and Why This Book Exists

Most people reach for support during divorce and discover that everyone has advice but no one has a plan. Divorce Bot is that missing plan. It is the second book in the Talk to Your Tools series, but you do not need to read the first book to understand how to use this one. Each title stands alone. Every book teaches you how to work with your AI partner with calm, clarity and strength.

AI is at its best when you give it a job. Your job here is simple. Tell your bot what you need. Use short sentences. Be direct. Ask follow-up questions. Ask for revisions. Ask for examples. You and your bot work together. Your guide. Your bot shapes information into clarity.

Divorce Bot does not replace the services of a lawyer or a therapist. It is your calm, organized, steady voice when your own mind feels scattered. It helps you think clearly.

It focuses on safety, stability and strength. It helps you manage the parts that feel overwhelming. There is nothing emotional in the structure. The power of this book lies in its ability to bring order to a time that feels chaotic.

This book is written to allow you to move through it at your own pace. If you are in crisis, start with Chapter Three.

If you are still deciding whether to stay or go, start with Chapter Two. If the marriage is already ending, begin with Part Two. You can jump around and return to any section as needed.

Your Divorce Bot is here to keep you steady. Divorce is not a single moment. It is a process. People often make costly mistakes when they act out of fear. This book walks with you so you can see the whole path ahead, one decision at a time.

You will learn:

- How to think clearly while your emotions swing
- How to protect your finances from day one
- How to communicate during conflict
- How to prepare for mediation or litigation
- How to keep records that protect you
- What steps to take each week
- How to rebuild once the papers are signed
- How to use your bot to plan your next life chapter

You are not alone. You have a tool that stays consistent, patient and organized even when everything else feels unstable. Let this book be your new starting point.

Let your bot guide you through hard moments and help you create the life that comes after.

Now we begin.

Chapter One

How to Work with Your AI Partner

Before you can use Divorce Bot effectively, you need to understand how to utilize ChatGPT. This chapter provides the fundamentals.

1. You must tell your bot what you want.
ChatGPT responds to direction. Be clear. Use simple instructions. You can say:
• "Rewrite this in a calmer tone."
• "Tell me the next three steps."
• "Summarize this in one paragraph."
• "Help me write a message that sounds firm but not angry."

2. Keep sentences short.
Your bot processes small, clear requests better than long paragraphs full of emotion or panic.

3. Ask follow-up questions.
Your bot expects you to ask again until you understand. This is not bothering the bot. This is the correct way to use the tool.

4. Give context.
If you provide your bot with a little background, it can offer you stronger and more accurate guidance. You can say:
• "I am worried about finances. What should I ask my lawyer?"
• "I am preparing for mediation next week. Help me organize my notes."

5. Use your bot as your second brain.
You can ask it to:
• Track what documents you need
• Help you prepare scripts for hard conversations

- Help you write emails
- Review your timeline
- Explain what to expect next
- Help you calm your thoughts when anxiety rises

6. You stay in control.
Your bot offers structure and clarity. You make the choices. You lead the direction.

7. You can return anytime.
Your bot does not forget, does not judge and does not rush. It waits for you to come back when you are ready to take the next step.

Divorce is emotional. Divorce Bot is not. That is the point. You need something steady when everything else feels uncertain. Now that you know how to use your tool, we can begin the work of understanding what your divorce will entail and how to navigate it with strength.

Chapter Two

When You First Realize the Marriage Is Ending

There is a moment when something shifts. It may be quiet. It may be loud. It may come after years of trying or come in one sharp instant. But you feel it. You know something is breaking. You know the marriage is no longer what you hoped it would be.

This chapter is for that moment.

You are not expected to be clear. You are not expected to be calm. You are not expected to have a plan. You only need to take one step at a time. Divorce Bot will help you think, organize, and understand what is happening without rushing you toward a choice. People make mistakes when they panic. You are here to avoid that.

Here is what you need to know in the first days.

1. Your feelings are information, not instructions.

You may feel angry, numb, relieved, or terrified. All of that is normal. Your emotions tell you that something important is happening, but they should not drive your decisions yet. Your job right now is to notice what you feel, not to act on it.

2. You do not have to announce anything.

Many people regret the first words they say when they are emotional. You do not have to tell your spouse anything today. You do not have to tell your children. You do not have to tell parents or friends. Right now, you gather information. You get steady. You breathe. You prepare.

3. You need clarity before action.

Ask Divorce Bot simple questions:

- "Help me name what I am feeling."
- "What questions should I ask myself before making a decision?"
- "What are the first signs that a marriage is truly ending?"
- "I am overwhelmed. Help me slow down."

Your bot will not judge your feelings. It will sort them.

4. You need privacy while you think.

Do not use shared devices. Do not store files in a location where others can access them. Do not leave searches open on home computers. Use your phone with a passcode. Use a private email if needed. This is not secrecy. This is safety.

5. You need a place to document the truth.

Open a notebook or a private digital file. Write down what is happening as plainly as you can. No emotion. Just facts. Dates. Times. Events. Your future self will need this record. This single step protects you more than you know.

6. You do not have to decide today if you are leaving.

People think divorce is a moment. It is not. It is a timeline. You can take weeks or months to understand what you want. You are allowed to stay while you figure out your next steps. You are free to leave at your convenience. Today is about knowledge, not decisions.

7. You can use Divorce Bot as a quiet space to think.

You can say:
- "Help me understand why I feel this way."
- "What signs show that a marriage cannot be repaired?"
- "What should I evaluate before deciding?"
- "Help me stay calm for the next hour."

When your mind feels loud, let the bot steady you.

8. You need to protect your energy.

Limit conversations with people who make you anxious. Do not argue. Do not explain. Save your strength for decisions that matter. Your emotional battery will be low right now. Guard it.

9. You are not failing.

Something in this relationship is no longer working. Seeing that clearly is a strength. Pretending everything is fine is what harms people. Awareness is the first step toward rebuilding a stable and peaceful life.

This chapter is about grounding yourself. Once you understand what is happening inside you, the next step is understanding what divorce looks like. Many people fear the unknown more than the divorce itself.

Chapter Three will give you the full map.

Chapter Three

What a Divorce Really Looks Like from Start to Finish

People talk about divorce as if it happens in a single moment. It does not. It unfolds in stages. When you understand the stages, you stop feeling lost. You stop reacting. You stop guessing. You move through the process with clarity, rather than fear.

This chapter provides you with the full map, so you always know what is coming next.

1. The Real Beginning: When One Person Mentally Leaves

Divorce starts long before anyone files paperwork.
It begins when one person quietly thinks, "I cannot do this anymore."

At this early stage, people often:
• disengage
• avoid hard conversations
• sleep less
• feel resentment building
• make private plans

If you are the person who mentally left first, you may feel guilty. If you are the person who discovers the shift later, you may feel shocked. Both experiences are common.

2. The Turning Point

There is a moment when thoughts turn into intention.
It may be triggered by an argument, a betrayal, a realization, or simply exhaustion. The turning point creates clarity. You understand that change is necessary.

During this stage, people often:

- gather documents
- start quiet research
- talk to trusted friends
- ask Divorce Bot for advice
- imagine life after separation

This stage is emotional. It is also productive. Intention brings control.

3. The First Actions

Once a person is certain, they begin taking concrete steps. You may:

- speak with a lawyer
- open a private email
- track finances
- document events
- look at housing options

Many people do not announce the decision yet because they want a plan in place first. This is practical, not deceptive. It prevents chaos.

4. The Conversation

This is the moment people fear most. The conversation where one person says, "I want a divorce."

It may be calm. It may be emotional. It may be explosive.
You cannot control someone else's reaction, but you can control the setting. Choose safety. Choose privacy. Choose a time without children present.

If speaking directly feels unsafe, you may choose to deliver the message with a counselor present or through your lawyer. Safety comes first.

5. The Temporary Phase

After the announcement, life enters a blurry stretch of transition. Both people are emotional. Both are uncertain. Daily routines shift.

During this period, people negotiate temporary arrangements for:
• living situations
• finances
• parenting time
• household responsibilities

This stage can feel chaotic. It will not last. It is the bridge between decision and structure.

6. Filing and Legal Steps

Once the divorce is formally filed, the process becomes structured. There are timelines, deadlines, and specific actions required.
Most divorces move through these steps:
• filing a petition
• receiving a response
• exchanging financial documents
• creating proposals
• mediation
• hearings if needed
• final agreement

The best approach is preparation. The worst is guesswork. Use Divorce Bot to ask questions along the way so you always feel informed.

7. Negotiation

This is where most divorces truly happen.
You and your spouse will work through:
• property division

- debts
- retirement accounts
- alimony questions
- custody schedules
- future decision-making plans

Effective negotiation is calm, clear, and grounded in documentation. Poor negotiation is emotional and reactive. This chapter prepares you to negotiate with strength, not fear.

8. Mediation or Litigation

Mediation is typically faster, less expensive, and more peaceful.
Litigation is necessary when someone refuses to cooperate or there are safety concerns.

Most divorces settle in mediation. A small percentage go to court.
You want to be the person who walks into mediation prepared, organized, and clear-headed.

9. The Final Agreement

This is the document that legally ends the marriage.
It states who gets what, who pays what, and how the children will be cared for. Once it is signed and approved, you are officially divorced.

It may feel emotional, but it also brings a sense of relief. The unknown becomes known. Your life becomes yours again.

10. After the Decree

This is the part nobody talks about enough.
After the paperwork is finished, you enter a new stage: rebuilding.

You may feel:

- sadness
- freedom
- anger
- relief
- confusion
- hope

All these emotions belong.

Life after divorce is not an ending. It is the beginning.

Chapter Four will help you understand the choices that come next and how to protect yourself as you move forward.

Chapter Four

Mediation vs Litigation**

Every divorce takes one of two paths.
You either work things out through mediation or you battle through litigation. One path saves money, time, and sanity. The other is necessary only when cooperation is impossible or safety is at risk.

This chapter explains both so you can choose the strongest option for your situation.

1. What Mediation Really Is

Mediation is a structured conversation guided by a neutral professional. The mediator does not take sides or make decisions. They help both people communicate, solve problems, and reach agreements.

Mediation is best when:
- both people can sit in a room without fear
- you want to save money
- you want to stay in control of decisions
- you prefer privacy
- you want a faster outcome
- you want to shield children from conflict

Mediation costs far less than going to court. It is not therapy. It is problem-solving.

2. What Mediation Feels Like

Most mediation sessions are calm and businesslike.
You sit at a table. The mediator outlines the topics. You talk through each one.

Typical topics include:
- parenting schedules
- money and debt
- retirements and savings
- property and vehicles
- the house
- future communication
- any ongoing support

The mediator keeps discussions on track. You will likely feel nervous at first. Everyone does. After a few minutes, the structure helps you settle.

3. Who Should Not Choose Mediation

Mediation is not appropriate if:
- there is a history of abuse
- one person intimidates the other
- one person hides money
- one person refuses to participate
- there is active addiction
- mental instability is affecting judgment

In these cases, mediation becomes unsafe or unfair. Litigation may be the only path.

4. What Litigation Really Is

Litigation means you and your spouse cannot reach an agreement on your own.
Each of you hires a lawyer. Your lawyers communicate for you. The judge makes the final decisions.

Litigation is best when:
• safety is an issue
• someone is manipulative or threatening
• someone refuses to negotiate
• someone hides assets
• the conflict is extreme

Litigation tends to be slow, expensive, and stressful, but it protects you when cooperation is impossible.

5. What Litigation Feels Like

Litigation is formal. You follow strict legal steps.
You may need to appear in court. You may give testimony. Your lawyer speaks on your behalf.

Common experiences in litigation:
• long timelines
• financial disclosures
• written statements
• hearings
• the judge setting deadlines
• high legal fees

Litigation feels less personal and more procedural. You may feel powerless at times. That is normal. Your lawyer becomes your shield.

6. How to Choose Between Mediation and Litigation

Use this simple guide:

Choose mediation when:
• there is basic cooperation
• you want control

• you want speed
• you want lower costs

Choose litigation when:
• you feel unsafe
• communication is impossible
• someone lies, hides money, or manipulates
• you need a judge to enforce fairness

Mediation is ideal for most couples. Litigation is a safety net for the rest.

7. How Divorce Bot Helps in Both Paths

You can use Divorce Bot to:
• prepare for mediation
• practice scripts
• organize documents
• understand legal terms
• plan your questions for your lawyer
• stay emotionally steady during conflict

The more prepared you are, the more confident you feel.

8. Your Goal

Your goal is not to "win."
Your goal is to create a fair agreement that allows you to move forward with stability and dignity.

Mediation gives you collaboration. Litigation gives you protection. Both lead to the same outcome: your new beginning.

Chapter Five will help you choose the right lawyer if you need one, and exactly what to look for when hiring someone to guide you.

Chapter Five

Choosing the Right Lawyer

If your divorce involves lawyers, the person you choose will shape the entire process. The right lawyer protects your future. The wrong one drains your energy, your wallet, and your peace.

This chapter helps you make a smart choice based on clarity, not fear.

1. What a Divorce Lawyer Really Does

A divorce lawyer:
- explains your rights
- guides you through required paperwork
- negotiates on your behalf
- protects you from manipulation
- helps you avoid costly mistakes
- represents you in court if needed

A lawyer is not your therapist. They are not your friends. They are professionals whose job is to safeguard your future.

2. What a Good Lawyer Feels Like

A good lawyer makes you feel:
- heard but not coddled
- informed but not overwhelmed
- respected, not judged
- calm, not frightened
- prepared, not confused

Your lawyer should speak plainly, answer questions directly, and give you realistic expectations.

3. Red Flags

Avoid any lawyer who:
- pressures you into conflict
- talks about "destroying" your spouse
- dismisses your concerns
- avoids explaining costs
- seems disorganized
- makes promises about outcomes
- gives you a bad gut feeling

Your lawyer should lower your stress, not add to it.

4. How to Interview a Lawyer

Schedule consultations with at least three lawyers.
Bring notes. Ask clear questions. Compare answers.

Questions to ask:
- How much experience do you have with cases like mine?
- What strategy would you recommend?
- What do you need from me right now?
- How do you communicate with clients?
- What will this likely cost?
- How can I keep costs down?
- What should I expect in the next 30 days?

A strong lawyer will give firm, clear answers.

5. Cost and Billing Basics

Lawyers usually bill by the hour.
Some may offer flat fees for certain tasks. Ask for a written fee agreement.

To keep costs manageable:
- stay organized
- respond quickly
- use email instead of long phone calls
- ask how to prepare documents yourself
- avoid emotional venting during paid time

You pay for every minute. Keep communication focused.

6. When You Need a Specialist

Choose a lawyer with extra experience if you have:
- high assets
- business ownership
- complicated custody issues
- international ties
- a spouse who hides money
- a history of abuse

Specialists understand complex cases and know how to protect you fully.

7. How Divorce Bot Helps You Prepare

Before meeting any lawyer, use Divorce Bot to:
- list your questions
- rehearse what to say
- gather your documents
- practice describing your situation
- create a simple timeline of events

The more prepared you are, the more value you get from each paid minute.

8. Your Goal

Your goal is not to find the "meanest" lawyer.
Your goal is to find the most effective one. Someone who is calm, organized, strategic, and skilled at negotiation.

The right lawyer makes everything smoother. The wrong one makes everything harder.

Chapter Six guides you through the basics of financial protection, providing the essential information you need before taking the next step.

Chapter Six

Financial Protection Basics

Money is a part of divorce that most people fear. That fear leads to rushed decisions, hidden details, and mistakes that echo for years. This chapter provides a clear foundation, enabling you to protect yourself without panic.

You do not need to be a financial expert. You only need to be organized and honest with yourself. Divorce Bot will help you do the rest.

1. Know Your Numbers

Before anything moves forward, gather the essentials:
• income (yours and your spouse's)
• monthly expenses
• bank accounts
• retirement accounts
• credit cards
• loans
• insurance policies
• tax returns

You cannot protect what you cannot see.

2. Make Copies of Everything

If you can access documents safely, make copies now.
Digital or paper is fine.
Store them in a private folder where your spouse cannot access them.

Collect:
• bank statements for the last 12 months

- tax returns for the last 3 years
- pay stubs
- mortgage statements
- car titles
- loan agreements
- investment records

You want a complete snapshot of your life before anything shifts.

3. Track Your Spending

For one month, observe your spending without judgment.
You are not trying to change anything.
You are trying to understand your life as it truly is.

This becomes important when:

- budgeting after divorce
- negotiating support
- explaining expenses to a lawyer
- making decisions about housing

Knowledge gives you leverage.

4. Understand Marital vs Personal Property

General guidelines:

- **Marital property** is what you acquired during the marriage.
- **Personal property** may include inheritances, gifts, or assets you owned before marriage.

In many states, even personal property can become shared if it was mixed with marital funds. If you have questions, note them. Your lawyer will explain your state's rules.

5. Open Your Own Accounts

Early in the process, you may want to:
- open a private checking account
- open a private savings account
- get a credit card in your own name

This gives you stability if shared accounts become unreliable or unsafe.

If you fear retaliation or financial control, take these steps quietly and safely.

6. Protect Your Credit

Divorce can damage your credit without you noticing.

To protect yourself:
- pull your credit report
- freeze your credit if necessary
- remove yourself from accounts you no longer use
- set up alerts on shared accounts

One missed payment on a shared card can haunt you.

7. If You Suspect Hidden Money

Do not accuse. Do not confront.
Just document what seems unusual.

Look for:
- sudden withdrawals
- new credit cards
- "forgotten" accounts
- missing statements
- cash transfers

• new business activity
• unusual purchases

Your lawyer or a financial professional can investigate if needed.

8. Use Divorce Bot to Get Organized

Divorce Bot can help you:
• list your accounts
• create a budget
• prepare questions for your lawyer
• sort your financial documents
• understand terms you do not know
• build a clear snapshot of your situation

Being organized makes you strong.
Being calm makes you strategic.
Being informed makes you less susceptible to manipulation.

9. Your Goal

Your goal is not greed.
Your goal is fairness, stability, and independence.

Once you understand your financial picture, you can make smart decisions in every chapter that follows.

Next up: **Chapter Seven: Protecting Your Income**.

Chapter Seven

Protecting Your Income

Your income is the engine of your independence.
If your marriage is ending, you must protect it early, calmly, and wisely.
This chapter walks you through the steps that keep you safe no matter what your spouse says or does.

1. Know Exactly What You Earn

Start with clarity.
List your income from every source:

- salary or hourly wages
- bonuses
- freelance work
- rental income
- side businesses
- government benefits

If anything is irregular, estimate conservatively.
This becomes the anchor of your financial plan.

2. Stop Sharing Private Work Information

Many spouses still share:

- pay stubs
- work emails
- office updates
- financial forecasts
- upcoming bonuses

You do not need to hide your life.
You do need to protect your stability.
Stop volunteering information that could be used against you.

3. Create a Private Digital Space

Set up:
• a private email
• a private folder for financial files
• a private notebook for documenting events

Do not store divorce-related information on shared devices or shared cloud accounts.

4. Prepare for Income Changes

Divorce can shift your financial reality overnight.
Ask yourself:
• If I needed to support myself alone, what would change?
• Where could I cut expenses if needed?
• Do I need additional work or freelance income?
• Should I update my resume?

You are not assuming failure.
You are preparing for stability.

5. If You Fear Jealousy, Retaliation, or Control

Some spouses react emotionally when income becomes separate.
Watch for:
• pressure to hand over paychecks
• demands to account for your spending

• attempts to sabotage your job
• arguments timed to disrupt your workday

If this happens, document everything.
Stay steady.
Do not engage in fights that could harm your work.

6. Protect Your Career

Your career is bigger than this divorce.

Take steps to protect it:
• keep your performance strong
• avoid letting personal drama spill into work
• resist the urge to vent to coworkers
• save proof of your achievements
• stay in good standing with your employer

You want to exit this process without losing momentum.

7. Track Your Time and Contributions

If you are the lower earner or a stay-at-home spouse, documenting unpaid labor becomes important.

Record:
• childcare
• household management
• emotional labor
• appointments
• budgeting

- eldercare
- support of your spouse's career

This establishes the real value you brought to the marriage and matters in negotiations later.

8. Anticipate Your Spouse's Claims

Some spouses attempt to rewrite history during the divorce process.

Common claims to expect:

- "You never contributed."
- "You spent all the money."
- "You don't need support."
- "You can earn more if you try."

Prepare your real story now.
Facts win, not accusations.

9. Let Divorce Bot Work for You

Divorce Bot can help you:

- calculate your monthly net income
- build a simple budget
- draft scripts for work-related boundaries
- organize your financial documents
- prepare questions about support or alimony

You do not need to hold everything in your head.
You only need to stay steady.

10. Your Goal

Your goal is not to "win."
Your goal is to remain stable, solvent, and self-reliant as your life transitions into its next chapter.

Next up: **Chapter Eight: Protecting Your Assets**.

Chapter Eight

Protecting Your Assets

When a marriage ends, emotions rise fast. Assets disappear fast, too. Protecting what you own is not about fear. It is about preparation and clarity.

This chapter provides the practical steps to secure everything that matters before the process becomes complicated.

1. Know What You Own

Start with an inventory.
List every asset, large and small.

Include:
- checking and savings accounts
- retirement accounts
- investment accounts
- cash on hand
- vehicles
- jewelry
- collectibles
- tools, equipment, or supplies
- real estate
- business interests
- digital assets
- inheritance property
- anything stored in a safe or storage unit

You cannot protect what you do not know exists.

2. Gather Proof of Ownership

Documents matter more than memories.

Collect copies of:
- titles
- deeds
- account statements
- insurance policies
- appraisals
- receipts
- screenshots of balances
- email confirmations of ownership

Store them safely in your private folder.

3. Separate Sentimental Items Early

Sentimental assets cause the biggest fights.
Gather and store your irreplaceables now.

This includes:
- family photos
- heirlooms
- letters
- childhood keepsakes
- artwork
- personal gifts

You do not have to hide them.
You do have to ensure they are safe.

4. Stop Adding Money to Shared Accounts

If you are considering divorce, stop funneling income into accounts that both of you can access.

Redirect deposits into an account in your name alone.
Keep the amount reasonable and traceable.
You are protecting stability, not hiding funds.

5. Watch for Disappearing Assets

If your spouse senses a change, assets may begin to shift.

Warning signs:
- cash withdrawals that "don't make sense"
- items disappearing from the home
- sudden credit card activity
- new safety deposit boxes
- transfers to relatives
- "business expenses" with no explanation

Document everything.
Patterns matter.

6. Photograph Everything of Value

Walk through every room and take photographs or videos.

Capture:
- serial numbers

- condition
- brand or maker marks
- collections
- equipment
- jewelry
- tools
- furniture

This creates a timestamped record that cannot be disputed later.

7. Know What Is Marital and What Is Not

Not all assets are treated the same.

Generally:
- Anything acquired during the marriage is marital.
- Anything you owned before the marriage may be separate.
- Gifts or inheritance given to you alone may remain yours.
- Improvements paid for with marital money may complicate things.

Divorce Bot can help you organize these categories for your lawyer.

8. Secure Your Digital Assets

Digital property is often forgotten and easily erased.

Protect access to:
- cloud storage
- digital photos
- online accounts
- cryptocurrency
- domain names

- software subscriptions
- creative assets
- business files

Change your passwords now.

9. Do Not Move Anything Big Without Advice

Hiding or transferring major assets before a divorce can backfire.

Before selling, transferring, or relocating anything of high value, speak with an attorney.
You want to be strategic, not impulsive.

10. Divorce Bot as Your Organizer

Use Divorce Bot to:
- build a full asset inventory
- create a list of documents still needed
- keep track of monthly balances
- prepare questions for mediation or legal consults
- generate scripts for financial conversations

You are not alone.
You are building a foundation for the rest of your life.

11. The Goal

The goal is simple:
Clarity, safety, and stability.
When your assets are protected, you can negotiate from a position of strength instead of fear.

Next up: **Chapter Nine: What To Do If You Own a Home Together**.

Chapter Nine

Protecting Your Income: What Must Happen Now

When a marriage ends, money becomes one of the sharpest pressure points. Not because people are greedy, but because income represents safety, stability, and the ability to keep life moving while everything else is changing. This chapter is about creating calm in the middle of that pressure.

You do not need to become a financial expert. You do need clarity, control, and simple systems. Divorce Bot helps you build all three.

1. Know your income down to the dollar
List every source of income you have, even the irregular ones. Salary, freelance work, side jobs, rental income, commissions, bonuses, Social Security, disability or VA payments, royalties, and anything seasonal. People often forget the small streams, but small streams add up.

2. Know your spouse's income
You need approximate numbers even if you do not have exact figures. Pay stubs, tax returns, bank deposits, and shared financial files are often the fastest way to learn what is real.

3. Separate what can be separated
If you have your paycheck deposited into a joint account, change that right now. Open a clean personal checking account in your name only. Do not move large sums. Simply redirect future deposits so your daily life does not depend on a joint pool of money.

4. Document any income manipulation

People sometimes shift income during divorce. They delay commissions, hide bonuses, change work status, or claim sudden financial hardship. If something feels off, make a note. Screenshot evidence. Save emails. Do not confront. Just record.

5. Protect yourself from sudden financial sabotage

Unfortunately, this happens. Accounts get drained, credit cards are maxed out, payroll deposits get "rerouted," or joint credit gets used to create chaos. Set up alerts on every account you can access. Daily notifications will save you from surprises.

6. Review your health insurance coverage

If you are covered under your spouse's plan, learn exactly what happens if you separate. Some plans drop coverage immediately once a divorce is filed. Others allow temporary continuation. Make a plan before you need one.

7. Start a simple emergency cushion

You need three things:

- cash you can reach
- money set aside for legal fees
- enough to cover basic bills if something gets disrupted

Even a small cushion helps you breathe.

8. Avoid "new debt panic spending"

Big emotional moments often lead to big emotional purchases. This is the time for calm, not for retail therapy or financial revenge. Every dollar you keep now is a dollar you will not need to fight to reclaim later.

9. Use Divorce Bot for your income map

Open a new note or document and record:

- every source of income
- where the money lands
- how it is used
- what needs to change

Once it is written down, you will feel steadier. Divorce does not knock you down. Lack of a plan does. You now have one.

Next: Chapter Ten

When this chapter is saved, you are ready to move into the most confusing part of divorce: understanding your assets and how to protect them.

Chapter Ten

Protecting Your Income: What Happens Next and How to Stay Steady

When a marriage ends, money becomes an emotional issue. It is charged with fear, anger, shame, hope, and every story you have ever believed about security. That's why protecting your income is one of the first serious steps in a divorce. It is not dramatic. It is not disloyal. It is simply wise.

This chapter gives you a steady plan.

1. Know your numbers today, not someday

Most people guess. They assume they know what they earn, what they spend, or what they will need. When divorce begins, guessing becomes expensive. Clarity is free.

Gather these essentials:

- Your most recent pay stubs
- A year of bank statements
- A year of credit card statements
- Any bonuses, commissions, or side-income history
- Health insurance deductions
- Retirement contributions
- Any automatic withdrawals you may have forgotten about

Write it down or record it. This becomes your starting point.

2. Separate the emotional from the practical

People confuse two completely different things:

- How they *feel* about money
- How money works

You may feel guilty. Angry. Terrified.
None of those feelings changes the math.

Your income is the engine that keeps you stable. The goal is not punishment or revenge. The goal is stability.

3. Stop the leaks
In almost every marriage, there are silent drains: subscriptions no one uses, automatic bills that were added years ago, perks one partner signed up for and forgot. Find them. Cancel them. Tighten your net so every dollar is accounted for.

This is not about scarcity. This is about control.

4. Understand what your income will look like during the divorce
Divorce can significantly alter your financial situation. You may face:

- Temp changes in living expenses
- Legal fees
- Mediation costs
- Child-related expenses
- Health insurance changes
- Temporary support orders

Most people are shocked by this shift because they are not prepared for it. You are preparing now. That puts you far ahead.

5. Don't make big moves yet
Do not quit your job, reduce your hours, switch careers, adjust your business structure, or make any dramatic income changes until you have clear legal guidance.

Courts do not like sudden income changes. They often interpret them as manipulative even when they aren't. Staying consistent protects you.

6. Understand your earning power
Your income today is not the full story. Courts look at:
• Your skills
• Your job history
• Your earning potential
• Your qualifications
• Your ability to return to work if you've been out of the workforce

Record your skills, your experience, and your strengths. If you need to job-hunt, reskill, or strengthen your résumé, Divorce Bot can help you do that step by step.

7. Build a simple income buffer
This is not emergency-fund perfection. This is practical:

Your goal is to set aside one month of expenses during the early stages.
Even $200 saved is better than nothing.
Momentum matters more than size.

You want the freedom to breathe, think, and not panic at every financial shift.

8. Document everything
Start tracking:
• Income received
• Money spent
• Shared expenses you cover
• Anything your spouse pays for
• Any sudden financial changes your spouse makes

Documentation is your shield. It strengthens your case, clarifies your negotiations, and reduces your stress.

9. Protect your work energy
Divorce takes emotional bandwidth. It is easy to let work slide. But your income is your independence. Protect your focus. Protect your projects. Protect your ability to perform.

You don't have to be perfect. You only need to be steady.

10. Your income is not just money. It is your freedom.
It is your power to choose.
It is your ability to walk away.
It is your proof to yourself that you will stand on solid ground.

Divorce Bot is going to walk with you through the next steps, one clear piece at a time. You're already doing the hardest part: staying present, staying organized, and staying steady.

Ready for Chapter Eleven whenever you are.

Chapter Eleven

Protecting Your Assets: What Stays Yours, What Gets Divided, and How to Stay Smart

When a marriage ends, assets become the battlefield people fear most. Houses, cars, savings, furniture, heirlooms, retirement accounts, collections, tools, antiques, art. All of it suddenly feels fragile.

But here is the truth most people never hear:
You don't need aggression.
You need clarity.

This chapter gives you a calm, structured way to protect what you own and prepare for what comes next.

1. Know what is "yours," what is "theirs," and what is legally "ours."

Emotion and law are not the same. You may feel something is yours because you picked it, paid for it, or used it. But legally, assets usually fall into three categories:

• *Separate property*: owned before the marriage, inherited during the marriage, or gifted specifically to you
• *Marital/community property*: anything acquired during the marriage, regardless of who paid for it
• *Mixed/commingled assets*: things that started separate but got blended over time

You don't need to solve the puzzle now. You just need to identify each piece.

2. Make a comprehensive list

List everything of value, and do it now before anything can be moved, "lost," or forgotten. Include:

- Bank accounts
- Investment and retirement accounts
- Real estate
- Vehicles
- Collections
- Tools, equipment, jewelry, luxury items
- Digital assets
- Business interests
- Cash-equivalent perks
- High-value furniture and antiques
- Insurance policies

Don't worry about accuracy yet. The first list is simply visibility.

3. Photograph everything

Walk through your home with your phone and record a slow video of each room, drawer, closet, cabinet, garage, attic, or storage area. Narrate what you see. This becomes timestamps and evidence if anything mysteriously disappears later.

This simple step has saved thousands of dollars for countless people.

4. Secure critical paperwork

Make digital or physical copies of:

- Deeds and titles
- Loan documents

- Insurance policies
- Tax returns
- Prenups
- Wills
- Trusts
- Business paperwork
- Anything showing ownership or value

Store copies in a secure folder, cloud storage, or a password-protected drive.

5. Freeze or restrict joint accounts only with legal guidance
People panic and start locking down accounts without understanding the consequences. In some states, that can create legal trouble. In others, it may be a good idea. The rules are simple:

Do not close or alter joint financial accounts until an attorney or mediator explains the safest timing.

6. Track shared spending from this point forward
Once divorce is on the horizon, every shared transaction matters.

Track:
- Who pays which bills
- Who makes large purchases
- Any sudden withdrawals
- Any new debt your spouse creates
- Any attempt to hide or move assets

You do not need to confront anyone. You only need to observe and record.

7. Understand emotional assets vs financial assets
Some assets feel priceless: the dining table you refinished, the antique ring, your grandmother's quilt, your art, your tools, your collections.

Others are just math: savings accounts, cars, and investments.

Divorce Bot rule:
Never trade long-term stability for short-term emotion.

If you keep a sentimental item, don't give up something financially crucial in exchange. You can replace furniture. You cannot replace retirement savings.

8. Don't move out with nothing
If you leave the home, bring the essentials you need—documents, medication, devices, chargers, and your personal valuables. Don't wait. Don't assume you can return freely later.

Take what is truly personal and leave everything else for the legal process.

9. Protect your credit
Your credit score becomes a lifeline after divorce.

Do this now:
- Pull your credit report
- Identify every account linked to your name
- Make sure nothing new is opened without your knowledge
- Turn on transaction alerts
- Consider freezing your credit if advised by your lawyer

10. Your assets are not just things
They are the history you built, the work you did, and the foundation you'll stand on next. Protecting them is not selfish. It is preparation.

You are not hoarding. You are stabilizing.
You are not fighting. You are planning.
You are not being dramatic. You are being wise.

When you handle your assets with clarity and calm, everything else becomes easier.

Ready for **Chapter Twelve** whenever you are.

Chapter Twelve

What to Do If You Own a Home Together

A shared home is the most emotional and financially complex asset in a divorce. It holds memories, routines, holidays, arguments, triumphs, disappointments, habits, and hopes. It is the backdrop of a life you built. And when the marriage ends, the home becomes the biggest question mark.

This chapter provides a clear and steady way to think through it.

1. Understand the three main paths
Most couples with a shared home do one of the following:

- *One person keeps the home and refinances it into their name*
- *The home is sold, and the equity is divided*
- *One person stays temporarily until finances are sorted*

Each path has emotional and financial consequences. There is no "right" one. There is only one that keeps you stable.

2. Step back from the emotion and look at the math
Almost everyone initially thinks:
"I want the house."
Or
"I need the house."

But ask yourself real questions:

- Can you afford the monthly payment alone?
- Can you qualify for a refinance?
- Can you maintain the home without resentment?

- Does staying help or hurt your emotional recovery?
- Is this a home or a symbol?
- Are you holding onto comfort or stability?
- Would downsizing give you more breathing room?

Divorce Bot rule:
If the house owns you more than you own it, let it go.

3. Gather the basic information immediately
You don't need legal guidance to start collecting these:

- The current mortgage balance
- The current interest rate
- The property tax amount
- The homeowners' insurance cost
- Any HOA dues
- Any major repairs needed
- The estimated current value

This provides you with the "home snapshot" that your lawyer or mediator will need.

4. If you want to keep the home
You will need to show:

- Proof of income
- Good credit
- Ability to refinance
- Ability to buy out your spouse's equity if required
- Ability to cover all future expenses

Many people discover that while they *love* the home, they cannot keep it without enormous financial strain. Letting go can be painful, but it can also be freeing.

5. If the home will be sold

Selling can be the cleanest and most neutral option.

Decisions you will need to make:

• Who chooses the real estate agent
• How repairs or staging costs are handled
• Whether both names stay on the mortgage until closing
• How the proceeds will be divided
• Whether one partner can stay until the sale is complete

Document all agreements in writing, even small ones.

6. If one person stays temporarily

This works when:

• You need stability for children
• You need more time to financially separate
• You're waiting on a refinance, sale, or income adjustment

Rules are essential:

• Who pays the mortgage
• Who pays utilities
• Who covers repairs
• How long the temporary arrangement lasts

Temporary arrangements without clear boundaries lead to conflict. Set the boundaries early.

7. Don't use the house as leverage or punishment
Many divorces become toxic because one person tries to use the home emotionally:
"You can't have this house."
"You're not leaving this house."
"I'll burn this place down before you get it."

The house is not the marriage.
The house is not a weapon.
The house is an asset.

Approach it like a business decision, not a battle.

8. Beware of "affordability denial"
People underestimate the cost of homeownership after divorce. Beyond the mortgage, there is:

- Maintenance
- Insurance increases
- Property tax increases
- Yard care
- Seasonal repairs
- Appliances breaking
- Unexpected emergencies

A house that once felt affordable with two incomes can become a heavy burden alone.

Home is not peace if it keeps you up at night.

9. Focus on your future home, not your past one
Where you live next is part of your new life. You get to choose what it looks like. Your next home could be:

- Smaller
- Brighter
- Simpler
- Closer to family
- In a new city
- A fresh space without old memories

Do not underestimate the emotional freedom that comes with a new address.

10. You cannot rebuild your life if you're drowning financially
Letting go of a home may feel like grief. But it can also be the doorway to breathing room, stability, and a future that isn't tied to the past.

You are not losing a home.
You are choosing a life.

Ready for **Chapter Thirteen** whenever you are.

Chapter Thirteen

Children, Custody, and Parenting Plans: Creating Stability in an Unstable Moment

Nothing makes a divorce feel more frightening than the thought of what happens to the children. Even in the calmest separations, this chapter becomes the emotional core. Parents fear losing time, losing influence, or losing connection. But divorce does not mean losing your children. It means reorganizing how you parent.

This chapter helps you do that with clarity, steadiness, and compassion.

1. The goal is stability, not perfection

Kids do not need perfect parents. They need steady ones. Divorce does not damage children. Conflict does. What protects them most is:

- predictable routines
- a calm environment
- honest communication
- two adults who are not using them as messengers or shields

If you can provide them with that, you are already ahead of most families going through divorce.

2. Know the three types of custody

Courts typically separate custody into two parts:

- *Legal custody*: who makes decisions about school, medical care, activities, religion, etc
- *Physical custody*: where the children physically live
- *Parenting time/visitation*: the structure of the schedule

Most modern courts prefer shared decision-making and consistent parenting time, unless there is a clear reason to the contrary.

3. Write down what your child needs, not what you want
This is the anchor for every plan.
Consider:

- age
- school schedule
- special needs
- relationships with extended family
- extracurricular activities
- medical requirements
- emotional temperament
- their need for downtime
- transportation logistics

Divorce Bot rule:
A good parenting plan is built around the child's life, not the parents' anger or convenience.

4. Create a child-centered schedule
There are many workable structures:

- Week-on/week-off
- 2-2-5-5
- 3-4-4-3
- Alternating weekends plus midweek visits
- One primary home with extended stays in the other

The best plan is the one that minimizes disruption, maximizes stability, and reduces the number of handoffs (a major stress point for kids).

5. Keep communication simple and neutral

You are not negotiating peace treaties. Use tools that lower the emotional temperature:

- shared calendar apps
- co-parenting apps with messaging logs
- written agreements for pick-ups and activities
- short, factual texts
- no sarcasm
- no surprises

Treat communication like business correspondence. Clear. Calm. Short.

6. Do not weaponize the schedule

Avoid making decisions based on:

- revenge
- leverage
- scoring points
- punishing your ex
- guilt
- fear

Kids notice everything. They know when a parent is using time as power. That leaves a mark that lasts longer than the divorce.

7. Protect your children's emotional world

You don't need a therapist to support your child. You need consistency. Use these guidelines:

- Never talk badly about the other parent
- Never use your child as a spy
- Never ask who they love more
- Never share adult information
- Never force them to choose sides

Kids should never carry adult weight.

8. Know the red flags that require legal protection

Your attorney or mediator needs to know if there is:

- substance abuse
- untreated mental health issues
- emotional or physical abuse
- financial instability
- neglect
- a history of violence
- dangerous living conditions

Not all situations are equal. Some require firm boundaries.

9. Build the plan that supports who your child will become

Your parenting plan affects their identity, confidence, and sense of home. Ask yourself:

- What environment makes them feel safest?
- Where do they thrive academically?
- What helps them stay connected to friends?
- What supports their emotional health?

Kids grow best in homes where they feel seen, valued, and heard.

10. Children are not dividing. Their life is expanding.
You are not tearing their world apart. You are teaching them resilience. You are showing them that adults can make hard decisions with grace. You are building a new version of family that can still be loving, steady, and whole.

You are not breaking your child's life.
You are building a different one that can be just as strong.

Ready for **Chapter Fourteen** when you are.

Chapter Fourteen

Communication Rules During Divorce

Divorce is not just a legal process. It is a communication crisis. People who once shared a life now struggle to share a sentence without misunderstanding or conflict. This chapter shows you how to communicate in a way that protects your sanity, your case, your finances, and your future.

These rules are simple. They are powerful. And they work.

1. Assume every word will be read by someone else
Judges. Lawyers. Mediators. Maybe even your children one day.
If you would be embarrassed to have it quoted in court, do not say it.

Divorce Bot rule:
Write every message as if you are sending it to an audience.

2. Keep all messages short
A good message is:

- brief
- factual
- neutral
- about logistics, not emotions

Example:
"Pickup today at 3:00. Let me know if anything changes."

That is enough. Long messages invite conflict.

3. Never send the message you wrote while angry
Divorce Bot technique:
Write it. Save it. Walk away.
Reread it one hour later. If your heart rate changes while reading it, do not send it.

Calm communication protects you far more than clever communication.

4. Use the BIFF method for difficult exchanges
BIFF stands for:

- Brief
- Informative
- Friendly
- Firm

It is the gold standard for dealing with emotional, manipulative, or combative ex-partners. You are not trying to win. You are trying to end the interaction quickly and cleanly.

5. Stay out of the emotional basement
Divorce conversations easily slip into:

- blame
- rehearsed arguments
- old wounds
- guilt trips
- accusations
- "you always" or "you never" statements

When the conversation drops into the past, climb out. Bring the focus back to the current task.

6. Do not negotiate while upset

Never make emotional agreements about:

- money
- custody
- property
- schedules
- living arrangements

People often say yes to something just to end the conversation, then regret it for years.

7. Neutral tone is your armor

No emojis. No sarcasm. No exclamation points.
Your tone should feel like a weather report.

Example:
"Tomorrow looks good. I will send the form at noon."

Neutral communication makes it harder for the other person to escalate.

8. Do not justify your decisions

You do not owe elaborate explanations.
Clear statements are enough.

"I cannot switch weekends this time."
"I will review the paperwork tonight."
"I would prefer to discuss this through email."

Explanations are invitations for arguments.

9. Protect your digital boundaries

This is one of the most overlooked areas.

• Do not allow late-night calls
• Do not respond instantly unless it's about the children
• Silence your phone during meals or rest
• No answering during emotional spikes
• No social media rants about your ex

Your peace matters.

10. Keep the focus on the future, not the past
Divorce is a forward-moving process.
Every conversation should point forward:

"What time works for you?"
"When can we exchange documents?"
"How do we keep this smooth for the kids?"

You cannot rewrite the past. You can write what comes next.

11. Remember: communication is evidence
Every calm message you send strengthens your credibility.
Every emotional message your ex sends strengthens your case.

Divorce Bot rule:
Let them create noise. You create the record.

12. Silence is a strategy
Not every message deserves a response.
Not every argument needs an audience.
Not every insult deserves a reply.

Strategic silence can be smarter than the perfect comeback.

Chapter Fifteen

How to Avoid the Most Expensive Mistakes

Divorce becomes financially dangerous not because people are careless, but because they are overwhelmed. Stress clouds judgment. Fear speeds decisions. Anger opens the door to choices that feel satisfying in the moment but cost thousands later.

This chapter provides a clear map of the pitfalls that drain money, time, and emotional energy. If you avoid these mistakes, you protect yourself more effectively than any courtroom strategy.

1. Making fast decisions just to "get it over with"

The most common financial disaster is agreeing too quickly.
People feel exhausted and say things like:

"I don't care, just take it."
"Fine, whatever you want."
"I just want this done."

These sentences create long-term regret.
Divorce Bot rule:
If the decision affects your housing, finances, retirement, or custody, it must not be made under emotional pressure.

2. Letting anger make your choices

Revenge is expensive.
If you fight only because you're furious, the lawyer fees pile up fast.

Do not choose:

- long court battles just to prove a point

• aggressive positions out of spite
• demands you don't need

Calm choices protect your bank account.

3. Not knowing what your assets really are
You cannot protect what you have not identified.

This includes:
• retirement accounts
• pensions
• investments
• cash savings
• valuables
• vehicles
• property
• business interests
• life insurance policies
• digital assets (yes, those matter now)

Make a full list before any negotiation. Missing items can cost you thousands.

4. Not understanding your debts
Divorce divides debt, too.
Many people are unaware that they remain legally responsible for debts even if their name is on the account, even if the ex-partner promises to pay.

Divorce Bot rule:
If your name is on it, you must protect it.

5. Failing to prepare for new expenses
Post-divorce life is often more expensive than expected.

You may have:
• new housing costs
• higher utilities
• new insurance
• child-related expenses
• transportation changes
• legal follow-up costs

A budget prepared now reduces panic later.

6. Using joint accounts for too long
The moment divorce begins, joint accounts become a source of danger. Money can disappear. Bills can be missed. Credit scores can be damaged.

The solution:
Separate accounts and clear tracking.

7. Mixing emotional and financial conversations
Never discuss money when emotions are running high.
Money requires a calm brain.

When the conversation feels heated, stop.
Say, "Let's continue this later," and step back.

8. Ignoring tax consequences
Some assets are not worth what they appear to be.
For example:
• Retirement accounts have withdrawal penalties.

- Selling a home may trigger taxes.
- Stocks have taxable gains.

Always compare assets, not just numbers.

9. Not keeping records
Documentation is protection.

Keep copies of:
- messages
- agreements
- financial statements
- receipts
- schedule plans
- anything promised verbally

In divorce, if it is not documented, it never happened.

10. Refusing professional help when you truly need it
DIY can save money until it doesn't.
Sometimes a consultation with a lawyer, accountant, or mediator prevents costly mistakes.

You don't need help for everything.
But you need it for the important things.

11. Letting guilt control your choices
Many people give away too much because they feel guilty about ending the marriage.
Guilt is not a financial plan.

Divorce Bot rule:
You are allowed to protect your future.

12. Forgetting to protect your credit
Your credit is a major source of stability.
Monitor it frequently during the divorce.
Unusual activity should be addressed immediately.

13. Not thinking long-term
Today you may feel tired, scared, or overwhelmed.
But someday this will be a memory, and your financial choices will still be with you.

Always choose the future over the moment.

Chapter Sixteen

Your Digital Life and Privacy

In modern divorce, your digital world is as important as your physical one. Phones, laptops, apps, cloud storage, car trackers, smart home devices, and shared accounts can all expose information, create vulnerability, or even be used against you.

This chapter shows you how to secure your digital life before problems appear.

1. Change every password immediately
Do not wait for signs of trouble.
Change passwords on:

- email
- banking apps
- social media
- cloud storage
- utilities
- online shopping accounts
- shared streaming services
- phone carrier accounts
- location-sharing apps

Use a new password you have never used anywhere else.

Divorce Bot rule:
Assume your ex knows your old passwords.

2. Protect your phone first

Your phone contains your entire world.
Update:

- lock screen code
- Face ID settings
- fingerprint permissions
- Apple ID or Google login
- backup locations
- text forwarding rules

If your ex ever had access to your devices, they may still be logged in somewhere.

3. Check for unknown devices or logins

Most platforms show where your account is signed in.

Look for:
- unfamiliar devices
- old devices you forgot about
- locations you do not recognize

Sign out everywhere. Then log back in only on the devices you currently use.

4. Turn off location sharing

Many people forget their phone is sharing their location with:
- their spouse
- their spouse's devices
- certain apps
- shared family plans

Turn off:
- Find My iPhone sharing
- Google location sharing
- Life360
- Snap Map
- Car GPS sharing
- Fitness trackers with shared activity

Where you go is your business now.

5. Watch your shared cloud accounts
iCloud, Google Drive, Dropbox, and shared photo albums can expose:

- private messages
- screenshots
- documents
- photos
- location history
- backups

If you shared a cloud account, separate immediately.

6. Secure your financial accounts
Logins to banks, PayPal, Venmo, Amazon, and credit cards may still be connected to shared emails or phone numbers.

Update:
- passwords
- two-factor authentication
- recovery phone numbers
- recovery emails

Two-factor authentication should go to **your** device only.

7. Review shared smart home devices

Smart homes can expose more than people realize.

Check:

- security cameras
- Ring doorbells
- Nest thermostats
- smart speakers
- shared Wi-Fi
- shared routers
- smart locks
- garage openers

If the device knows your schedule, so does your ex.

8. Clean up social media

Do not announce the divorce.
Do not post emotional content.
Do not "subtweet."
Do not share quotes about betrayal, rebirth, or freedom.
Do not post photos that invite commentary.

Social media screenshots become evidence.

Divorce Bot rule:
During divorce, social media is a museum of silence.

9. Stop using shared devices

If there is a laptop or tablet you both once used, treat it as unsafe.

It may contain:
- old passwords
- saved logins
- browser histories
- synced messages
- keyloggers
- tracking programs

Use only your own side of the digital world.

10. Protect your email
Your email is the key to everything—legal documents, financial updates, court notices, and attorney communication.

Steps:
- Change the password
- Enable two-factor authentication
- Remove recovery contacts
- Create folders for divorce communication
- Turn off text message forwarding

If your email is open, your entire life is open.

11. Track your credit
Digital tampering often shows up as:
- new accounts opened in your name
- credit card applications
- credit checks
- unusual purchases
- changes to account details

Use a credit monitoring tool or check manually each month.

12. Do not snoop on your ex's digital world
Even if you have access.
Even if you have the password.
Even if you are tempted.

Snooping is illegal and can damage your case.

Focus on securing your side, not invading theirs.

13. Save everything relevant
Without being sneaky or hacking, save:

- calendars
- income records
- joint account statements
- tax records
- important emails
- messages about agreements
- screenshots of significant conversations

Digital order creates legal strength.

14. Do not discuss your strategy through insecure channels
Never talk about:

- your lawyer
- your plans
- your fears
- your evidence
- your finances

through shared emails, shared Wi-Fi, or devices you don't fully control.

Use only trusted, private devices for sensitive communication.

15. Your digital life is part of your protection
People underestimate how many divorce battles are won or lost because of digital mistakes.

Securing your digital world is not paranoia.
It is preparation.

Chapter Seventeen

When You're Being Manipulated

Not every divorce turns ugly. Many do.
Manipulation during divorce does not always look like shouting, threats, or dramatic outbursts. Often it is subtle. Quiet. Familiar. It feels like the same emotional patterns that were present in the marriage—only stronger.

This chapter teaches you how to recognize manipulation instantly and stop it before it drains your energy, money, and confidence.

Manipulation thrives in confusion.
Divorce Bot exists to give you clarity.

1. The guilt strategy
This one sounds like:

"I can't believe you're doing this."
"After everything I've done for you."
"You're breaking up the family."
"I guess none of it meant anything to you."

This is not love.
This is control.

Guilt is meant to make you question your right to protect yourself.
You do not owe guilt payments to anyone.

2. The pressure cooker
This shows up as:

"Answer me right now."
"I need a decision today."
"If you don't respond, I'll assume you agree."

Pressure is used to create panic, so you'll surrender something important.

Divorce Bot rule:
If someone insists you act fast, slow down.

3. The sudden kindness
Manipulative people often switch from anger to sweetness overnight.

"I've been thinking… maybe we can work this out."
"You're still the most important person in my life."
"I miss you."

If this happens unexpectedly, be cautious.
Kindness can reopen doors that they want control over again. It can also prevent you from taking necessary steps, such as gathering documents or meeting with a lawyer.

Kindness is real when it is consistent, not strategic.

4. The financial fog
This is the act of keeping you confused:

"I'll handle the money. Don't worry about it."
"There's nothing you need to see."
"You don't understand how this works."

Financial fog is deliberate.
It keeps you from knowing your rights.

When someone minimizes your access to information, they are protecting themselves, not you.

---

5. The memory rewrite

This sounds like:

"That never happened."
"You're overreacting."
"You're imagining things."
"You're remembering it wrong."

This is gaslighting.
If you have documents, messages, screenshots, or numbers, trust the evidence—not the rewrite.

6. The emotional ambush

Manipulators pick the moment when you're tired, lonely, or overwhelmed to bring up big issues:

late at night
during stressful days
right before major events
during children exchanges
after emotional conversations

This timing is intentional.
When your brain is tired, you are more likely to agree to something you shouldn't.

7. The martyr routine

This is dramatic self-pity:

"I'm the one suffering here."
"I guess I'll be alone forever."
"Everyone will blame me."

The goal is to make you feel responsible for their emotional stability.

You are not responsible.

8. The blame shift

Manipulators rarely stay in one role for long.
They shift from victim to hero to victim again.

Everything becomes your fault.
Even their behavior.
Even their choices.

This is not a negotiation.
It is an emotional trap.

9. The "you owe me" tactic

This one tries to attach your past to your future.

"I supported you when…"
"You wouldn't have anything without me."
"You owe me after all I've done."

You do not owe anyone your future.

10. Isolation attempts

They may try to separate you from support:

"Don't talk to your friends about this."
"You're getting bad advice."
"You should stop listening to other people."

Isolation is one of the strongest signs of manipulation.
Support is your protection.

11. Testing your boundaries
Manipulators push boundaries slowly:

one extra message
one inappropriate comment
one schedule change
one guilt trip

If you allow small things, they can escalate into big things.

Firm boundaries are essential.

12. The "good parent" performance
If children are involved, manipulators sometimes use them as props to appear compassionate or cooperative.

"I'm doing this for the kids."
"The kids want to stay with me."
"You're hurting the kids by doing this."

Document everything.
Emotional performance is not parenting.

13. The fear lever
Fear statements sound like:

"You'll lose everything."
"You can't afford to leave."
"No one will help you."

Fear is a lever used to keep you stuck.
The truth is usually far less dramatic.

14. How to protect yourself

The antidotes to manipulation are simple:

- clear boundaries
- documentation
- neutral communication
- no rush decisions
- support from trusted people
- calm strategies
- focusing on facts, not feelings

Divorce Bot rule:
Once you recognize manipulation, it loses its power.

15. You are not powerless

Manipulation works only when you do not see it.
Now you see it.
Now you can stop it.

You are allowed to be strong.
You are allowed to be clear.
You are allowed to walk away from emotional traps.

You are not alone in this process—your clarity is growing page by page.

Chapter Eighteen

Staying Strong During the Process

Divorce is not just a legal event.
It is an endurance test of the mind, the heart, and the nervous system.
Even when the decision is right, the process can shake you. This chapter teaches you how to stay steady, grounded, and clear from the first filing to the final signature.

You are not meant to "power through" alone.
You are meant to stay strong with structure, support, and strategy.

1. Strength is not toughness
Many people confuse strength with pretending nothing hurts.
Real strength looks different. It is:

clear thinking
calm action
steady boundaries
good sleep
healthy routines
honest conversations with yourself

Strength is not loud.
It is consistent.

2. Your nervous system needs support
Divorce is one of the top stress events in a lifetime.
Your body reacts even when your mind tries to stay calm. You may notice:

tension in your jaw
racing thoughts
cold hands
tight chest
forgetfulness
fatigue
restlessness
irritability

This is not a weakness.
This is biology.

Support your nervous system with simple habits:

short walks
A glass of water every hour
deep breathing before any legal conversation
a bedtime ritual
quiet mornings before you check your phone

These small habits stabilize you more than you think.

3. Build a steady routine
During divorce, structure becomes strength.
Routines reduce uncertainty, and uncertainty is one of the biggest emotional drains.

Try this:

morning: one grounding activity
midday: one action toward your future (emails, documents, planning)
evening: one calming habit (reading, stretching, journaling)

You do not need to fix everything today.
You only need steady steps.

4. Limit emotional exposure

Every conversation does not deserve a reaction.
Every message does not require immediate response.

Use this rule:
If it's emotional, wait.
If it's legal, document.
If it's urgent, stay brief.

Limit long text threads, late-night discussions, and circular arguments.
These drain your strength more than anything.

5. Protect your energy from other people's opinions

Everyone has something to say about divorce:

"Fight for everything."
"Be kinder."
"You should leave."
"You should stay."
"You need a better lawyer."
"You're moving too fast."
"You're moving too slow."

But you are the one living this, not them.

Listen to advice, but follow your own compass.

6. Choose your support team

A good support team is not a giant circle of people.
It is a small, reliable group of:

one practical friend
one emotional friend
one legal expert
one financial guide
one calming person who speaks truth, not drama

These people hold you up when your energy dips.

7. Do not measure your strength by your bad days

You will have days where you feel clear and powerful.
You will have days where you feel tired and emotional.

Both days count.

Strength is not about being perfect.
It is about continuing.

8. Stay occupied with your own future

Divorce shrinks your focus to problems.
To stay strong, you need to expand it again.

Work on things that remind you who you are:

projects
learning
creative work
walking outside
new routines

reading
volunteering
planning a future space or trip

A future is not something you wait for.
It is something you build piece by piece.

9. Give your mind something to hold onto
When you feel overwhelmed, anchor yourself with:

"I am allowed to protect my peace."
"I do not need to respond right now."
"I am moving forward even if today feels slow."
"I deserve calm."

These short truths keep you grounded when emotions surge.

10. Let go of the guilt that does not belong to you
Many people feel guilty during divorce even if they did nothing wrong.
Guilt is often used as a tool against you, or it creeps in from old patterns.

Release guilt that is borrowed, inherited, or placed on you by others.

You are allowed to choose a healthier life.

11. Strength comes from clarity
Know your priorities:

protect yourself
protect your finances
protect your home
protect your documents
protect your peace

Let everything else fall behind those priorities.

12. Celebrate small wins
Did you fill out a form?
Send an email?
Stay calm?
Organize one drawer?
Walk for ten minutes?
Eat a real meal?

These count.
Small wins are how big wins get built.

13. Remember who you are outside of this divorce
You are not defined by this process.
You are a whole human with skills, memories, dreams, talents, friends, stories, plans, humor, creativity, and possibility.

Divorce does not shrink your identity.
It clears space for your actual life to grow.

14. You are getting stronger every day
Even when you don't feel it.
Even when the paperwork feels endless.
Even when the emotions rise.
Even when you are tired.

You are building a version of yourself that is steady, clear, and unshakeable.

Divorce Bot's purpose is to get you there with clarity, compassion, and strength.

Chapter Nineteen

When It Finally Ends

The end of a divorce does not arrive with trumpets or confetti. It often comes in an email from your lawyer, a quiet court document, or a moment where you suddenly realize you have nothing left to sign.

After months or years of emotional pressure, the finish line can feel strangely calm. You may expect a wave of joy, but what arrives first is usually release.

This chapter prepares you for that moment, the hours after, and the days that follow.

1. The moment the paperwork is final

The end of a marriage fits into one short message:

"The judge signed it."
"It has been filed."
"You're officially divorced."

It feels surreal.
You may stare at the message longer than you expect.
You may read it three times.
You may feel nothing at first.

Do not judge your reaction.
This moment is personal.

2. The first emotions

People imagine they will feel:

relief
joy
freedom
victory

And sometimes they do.
But just as often, the first emotions are mixed:

numbness
sadness
exhaustion
confusion
unexpected quiet

This is normal.
You've been running a marathon in your mind for a long time.
Your body finally gets permission to rest.

3. You may grieve the idea, not the person
Many people feel sadness because they are grieving:

who they hoped their partner would be
what the marriage could have been
the life they imagined
the time invested
the version of themselves they were during that chapter

This grief does not mean you made the wrong decision.
It means you cared deeply and you are human.

4. The identity shift

When the legal ties break, the emotional ties begin to rearrange.
You may notice:

the house feels different
your routines feel different
your weekends feel open
your phone feels strangely quiet
your dinner table feels symbolic
your name (if changed) feels like a step into a new room

These sensations are normal.
Identity shifts quietly and slowly, not in a single day.

5. The physical crash

Many people feel tired for weeks after their divorce finalizes.
This is the post-adrenaline drop.
Your nervous system has been on high alert for so long that the quiet feels unfamiliar.

Rest is not a luxury.
It is medicine.

6. The urge to do something dramatic

After divorce becomes official, some people want to:

cut their hair
buy new furniture
move houses
go on a trip
start dating immediately

tell everyone
tell no one

Before you make big changes, pause.
Give yourself a few days to settle.
Let your system balance.

Big life choices land better from a clear mind.

7. You may want closure from the wrong place
You may want one final conversation, apology, explanation, or acknowledgment.

Most people never get it.
And that is still closure.

Closure is a decision you make, not a gift they give.

8. The documents you need to secure
Now that the divorce is final, you need to organize your:

final decree
property division documents
parenting plan
support agreements
updated will
updated beneficiaries
updated insurance
updated passwords
updated legal name documents (if applicable)

This is the administrative side of closure.
It gives you a foundation for your new life.

9. The moment your home becomes your home again
Your space will feel different now.

Some people immediately remove items that hold emotional weight.
Others take a slower approach, one drawer at a time.
Both are valid.

Your home becomes yours again when you decide it is.
Not when every trace of the past is gone.

10. The relationships that shift
Some people may drift away.
Some may stay closer than ever.
Some may surprise you with kindness.
Some may reveal their true nature.

Let these shifts unfold without forcing anything.
You are entering a new chapter.
Your relationships will align with who you are now, not who you were then.

11. Give yourself one symbolic act
A symbolic act helps your mind recognize the new beginning.

You could:

write a letter you never send
light a candle and breathe
take a walk and let something go

clean one drawer
change your sheets
buy a new plant
delete old messages
create a small ritual of your own

Symbolic acts turn emotional transition into something you can see and touch.

12. The first night

The first night after the divorce is often quiet.
You may feel fragile.
You may feel powerful.
You may feel nothing at all.

All of these are real.

Do something gentle:

make a warm meal
take a bath
put on a favorite show
read something comforting
go to bed early

This night does not define your future.
It simply marks the end.

13. The morning after

You wake up and realize something is different.
Your mind starts scanning for the old stress.

But it is not there.
There is space.

This is your first morning in your new life.

14. You are not starting over
You are not back at zero.
You are moving forward with:

experience
clarity
strength
identity
lessons
possibility

You are not starting over.
You are starting fresh.

15. The quiet power of your new freedom
Freedom is not loud.
It is subtle.
It is the ability to make decisions without conflict.
It is the ability to rest without tension.
It is the ability to breathe without fear.

This is the reward at the end of the road.

16. What comes next
What comes next is Part Three of this book.
A clear path.
A clean slate.

A strong rebuild.
A future that belongs entirely to you.

And Divorce Bot walks with you into that future.

Chapter Twenty

How to Rebuild Your Life

When the divorce is final, you stand in a quiet space between what was and what comes next. This chapter provides a framework for rebuilding. Not rushing. Not reinventing yourself overnight. Rebuilding with clarity and intention.

The goal is simple.
You build a life that fits you now.

1. Begin with the truth
Your first step is simple:

Admit to yourself that the old life is over.

Not in a dramatic way.
Not with sadness or celebration.
Just honesty.

You cannot rebuild until you accept that you are no longer living through the story that led to this moment. Once you accept it, the path forward gets wider.

2. You rebuild in phases
People think rebuilding is a single project.
It is not.
It is a sequence:

stabilize
organize
recover

dream
create
grow

Trying to skip a phase makes the process harder.
Follow the sequence and you will feel steady instead of scattered.

3. Stabilize: Your first 30 days
Rebuilding starts with the basics.

sleep
hydration
gentle movement
regular meals
financial essentials
calendar organization
clear communication boundaries
tidying small parts of your home

This first phase is about giving your brain and nervous system a safe foundation. Nothing else works without it.

4. Organize: Your next 30 days
Once you are stable, you begin to organize your life.

sort your paperwork
clean your car
organize your bedroom
refresh your bathroom
update digital accounts

refresh your closet
rewrite your daily routines

You do not need to become a new person.
You simply create order.
Order creates strength.

5. Recover: Your next 60 days
This is where emotional healing begins in earnest.

Some people talk to a therapist.
Some talk to friends.
Some journal.
Some walk.
Some create.
Some sit quietly.

You do not have to pick the same method every day.
You choose whatever helps you move the feelings through your system.

Recovery is motion.
Not speed.
Motion.

6. Dream: Your next 30 days
Once you feel steadier, your mind begins to open.

This is where you ask yourself:

What do I want now
What do I want my days to feel like
What have I always wanted to try

What parts of myself did I lose
What parts of myself do I want to grow

Dreaming gives you direction.
You are not deciding your future yet.
You are locating your desires.

7. Create: Your next 90 days
This is the most exciting phase.

You take the dreams you've identified and turn them into small, manageable actions.

If you want friendship, you join one community activity.
If you want fitness, you start with ten-minute walks.
If you want creativity, you pick one project.
If you want confidence, you try one new thing a week.
If you want joy, you schedule it instead of waiting for it.

Creation is the act of becoming.

8. Grow: Your next year
Growth is where your new life becomes your real life.

It is the slow layering of:

skills
habits
relationships
stability
self-trust
joy

peace
new stories

This is where the transformation becomes visible.
You begin to feel like yourself again.
Then you begin to feel like someone even stronger.

9. Give yourself milestones, not deadlines
Deadlines create pressure.
Milestones create momentum.

Use milestones like:

"I will organize my bedroom this month."
"I will update my résumé by next Friday."
"I will take one new class this quarter."

Milestones keep you moving without stress.

10. Rebuild your social circle intentionally
Divorce changes your social landscape.

Some relationships will strengthen.
Some will fade.
Some will reveal their true character.

Focus on building:

three people you trust
three people who support your growth
three people who appreciate your life now

You do not need a crowd.
You need a core.

11. Let joy return gently
Joy often returns in small sparks:

a clean kitchen
a conversation with someone new
a morning without anxiety
a night where you sleep deeply
a meal you enjoy
a walk that clears your mind
a laugh that surprises you

Pay attention to these sparks.
They are the beginning of your new emotional landscape.

12. Redesign your identity on purpose
You get to decide who you are now.

Are you adventurous
Are you creative
Are you peaceful
Are you bold
Are you romantic
Are you independent
Are you rebuilding your confidence
Are you trying something new

You are not limited by your past.
You are shaped by your choices.

13. Rebuild your confidence from the ground up

Confidence is built through:

competence
consistency
courage

Small wins create a strong spine.
Do five-minute tasks.
Take one small risk.
Celebrate the tiniest progress.

Confidence grows like a muscle.
Regular use makes it strong.

14. Create financial clarity

Financial stability increases emotional stability.

Track your spending
Update your budget
Set goals for saving
Pay down one small debt
Open a separate emergency fund
Review insurance
Review retirement basics

You do not need wealth to feel secure.
You need clarity.

15. Redefine your home

Your home is not a museum of your past.
It becomes your sanctuary again when you:

move furniture
add new bedding
change the lighting
add plants
hang new art
clean one neglected corner

Small changes transform the energy of a space.

16. Return to your body
Your body has held tension for a long time.

Release it through:

stretching
massage
long walks
yoga
swimming
gentle strength training

Your body deserves care.
You deserve comfort.

17. Forgive yourself first
Forgiveness is not letting anyone else off the hook.
Forgiveness frees your energy.

Forgive yourself for:

staying too long
trying too hard

not knowing what you know now
wanting peace
choosing yourself

Self-forgiveness is the highest form of self-respect.

18. You rebuild by becoming someone you trust

Rebuilding your life is not the process of becoming someone new.
It is the process of becoming someone you trust.

Someone who keeps promises to themselves.
Someone who chooses well.
Someone who sees the truth.
Someone who protects their own peace.
Someone who knows their worth.

19. This chapter ends where your new life begins

Your past is behind you.
Your future belongs to you.
Your next steps will shape everything from here.

And Divorce Bot walks with you through each one.

Chapter Twenty-One

How to Rebuild Your Life After Divorce

When the dust settles, there is a moment when the world feels too quiet. The court dates are behind you. The arguments are over. The paperwork is done. The adrenaline drops. And suddenly you are left with yourself again.

This chapter guides you through what happens next.
Not the dramatic version.
The real version.

Your life is not starting over.
Your life is continuing.
And you get to shape it with care.

1. Accept that life after divorce is a process
There is no single day when everything clicks into place.
Life after divorce unfolds in stages. You may feel strong one week and shaky the next. This is normal. You are not going backward. You are recalibrating.

2. Rebuild your routines first
Before you tackle big dreams, rebuild the rhythm of your day.

wake up at a consistent time
take care of basic tasks
simplify meals
clean one small space a day

put important dates on a shared calendar
create one simple nightly routine

Structure stabilizes your emotions.
Chaos makes healing harder.

3. Give yourself permission to slow down
People often rush into new relationships, new projects, new goals. They want a distraction from the quiet. Slow down instead. Healing requires space. Clarity arrives when the noise fades.

4. Start with small wins
Do not rebuild your whole life at once.
Pick a tiny, doable task. Finish it.

make your bed
clear your nightstand
organize one drawer
write one bill payment on your calendar

Small wins create momentum.

5. Create a vision for your next chapter
Ask yourself:

What do I want my life to feel like
What values matter to me now
What habits support the person I want to become
What relationships energize me
What relationships drain me

You are not answering for your old life.
You are answering for your future.

6. Refresh your physical space
A new environment supports a new mindset.
You do not need to redecorate your home.
You just change the energy.

wash your bedding
add a lamp
buy a plant
move a chair
add a new scent
paint a wall
replace one object that reminds you of the past

Your surroundings influence your emotional stability more than you realize.

7. Build your independence muscles
Many people emerge from marriage feeling uncertain about handling everyday tasks on their own.
That is okay.
You build independence by doing.

learn one new skill each month
update your financial literacy
plan a small solo outing
repair one thing in your home
cook a meal you have never made before

Each step teaches you that you can rely on yourself.

8. Rebuild your friendships and social circle
Some relationships will fade after divorce.
Some will surprise you with loyalty.
Some will step forward for the first time.

Focus on finding people who:

listen without judgment
support your growth
do not feed drama
respect your boundaries

Quality matters more than quantity.

9. Reinvent joy
Your joy will not return the same way it used to.
It comes back in unexpected places.

a book you cannot put down
a walk that clears your mind
a new restaurant
a night of peaceful sleep
a new class or hobby
a road trip

Joy returns in pieces. Collect them.

10. Rebuild your financial confidence
Divorce rearranges finances.
Here is how you regain footing.

get a clear snapshot of your income, bills, and debt
set one short-term money goal
open or update your savings account
start an emergency fund
cut two non-essential expenses
review retirement basics

Financial clarity increases emotional peace.

11. Heal your body from the stress
Divorce is hard on the nervous system.
You may feel exhausted for months.
Your body needs recovery.

long walks
stretching
sleep hygiene
hydration
massage
gentle strength training
breathing exercises

Healing is physical as much as emotional.

12. Let yourself grieve without shame
Grief is not a sign that you made the wrong decision.
Grief is what happens when a chapter ends.

You grieve expectations.
You grieve routines.

You grieve the person you used to be.
You grieve the version of the marriage you hoped for.

Let the feelings come.
They do not last forever.

13. Be careful with new relationships
You do not need to swear off love.
You just need to choose it thoughtfully.

Do not date to fill a void.
Do not date to feel validated.
Do not date because you feel pressured.
Date when you feel steady enough to make healthy choices.

Healthy relationships are built on clarity, not loneliness.

14. Celebrate your progress
Rebuilding is made of small moments.

your first peaceful week
your first morning you wake up smiling
your first financial breakthrough
your first new friendship
your first organized room
your first day you feel excited about the future

Celebrate all of it.
Those moments matter.

15. You are not starting over. You are moving forward.
Divorce does not erase your life.
It redirects it.

Your skills
your wisdom
your strength
your history
your dreams
your identity

They all come with you.
And they will shape a future that feels strong, capable, and fully yours.

When you rebuild after a divorce, you become someone you can trust.
And that is the most powerful outcome of all.

Chapter Twenty-Two

Protecting Your Income

When a marriage ends, money becomes one of the most significant factors affecting your financial stability. Emotions run high, decisions get rushed, and people often make mistakes that cost them years of financial security. You do not need to become a finance expert to protect yourself. You just need clear steps, steady thinking, and a commitment to keeping your future safe.

This chapter focuses on the practical actions that protect your income right now and in the months ahead.

1. Get a complete picture of your income

Before you protect anything, you must know exactly what money is coming in.

your paycheck
side income
benefits and bonuses
retirement contributions
alimony or support you already receive or pay

Open a new document and record everything.
Clarity is the foundation of control.

2. Open your own bank account immediately

If you do not already have a personal account, open one today.
This is not disloyal or dramatic.
It is responsible.

Use this account for:

your paycheck
your savings
your emergency fund

This ensures you always have access to your own money.

3. Direct your paycheck into your personal account
As soon as possible, update your direct deposit.
Money that goes into a joint account can be frozen, drained, or monitored.
Protecting your income starts with routing it somewhere safe.

4. Stop using joint credit cards
Joint debt is shared debt.
Even if your spouse racks up the bill, creditors can come after you.

Cut off spending on joint cards immediately.

close or freeze accounts when allowed
request your own card with a separate line
track anything your spouse charges

Protecting your credit protects your income.

5. Update online passwords
Your spouse does not need to know or access your financial identity.

change passwords for banks
email
cloud storage

shopping sites with stored payment methods
financial apps

Your digital life is part of your income protection plan.

6. Save aggressively during this transition
The first months of separation are expensive.

lawyers
temporary housing
furniture
unexpected bills
court fees

You need a cushion while things shift.

Aim to build a simple emergency fund equal to one month of income.
It does not need to be perfect.
It just needs to exist.

7. Track your spending for one week
You do not need a full budget yet.
You just need awareness.

Write down everything you spend for seven days.
Patterns will appear quickly.

This helps you:

spot waste
slow emotional spending
prepare for life on one income
identify what to cut or keep

Awareness saves money.

8. Protect your job and professional reputation
Many people underestimate the impact divorce has on work.
Stress makes you distracted.
Court dates interrupt your schedule.
Emotions drain your focus.

Tell one trusted person at work if needed.
Keep communication simple and professional.
Document everything that affects scheduling.
Guard your reputation with intention.

Your income depends on your stability.

9. Prevent your spouse from sabotaging your financial life
Most divorces do not involve sabotage, but some do.
Prepare for the possibility.

watch joint accounts daily
print or save statements
document anything unusual
freeze joint lines of credit if allowed
remove automatic payments you rely on

You are not being paranoid.
You are being cautious.

10. Know your rights regarding temporary support
Depending on your state and situation, you may qualify for temporary financial support during separation.

Do not assume either way.
Ask a lawyer or mediator directly.

Temporary support exists to prevent immediate harm.
Use the help if the law allows it.

11. Avoid quitting your job or reducing your hours
Some people make big changes during emotional moments.
Do not reduce your income until your divorce is finalized.
Courts look closely at income changes.
A sudden drop can affect support calculations and future stability.

Hold steady until you have legal clarity.

12. Document everything related to money
Documentation protects you more than emotion ever will.

log conversations about money
keep receipts
save emails and screenshots
record dates when accounts were changed
print key financial papers

Facts speak louder than stories.

13. Use ChatGPT to stay organized and informed
This book comes with a built-in advantage.
Your bot can help you protect your income.

ask it to track your spending
ask for scripts to handle financial conversations
ask it to explain complex terms

ask it to draft emails to your bank
ask it to help create your emergency budget

Your ChatGPT partner is your calm financial assistant.

14. Create a simple short-term money plan
You do not need a full budget right now.
You just need control.

income this month
essential bills
court or legal expenses
gas, food, and necessities
one small amount for personal care
a savings target

A short-term plan keeps you out of crisis mode.

15. Remember that protecting your income is protecting your future
This is not about greed or fear.
This is about survival and stability.

When you protect your income, you protect:

your housing
your food
your health
your children
your independence
your future choices

Money is not the whole story of divorce, but it is the backbone of your next chapter.

You are not just protecting numbers.
You are protecting the life you are about to build.

Chapter Twenty-Three

What To Do If You Own a Home Together

A shared home is one of the biggest stress points in any divorce.
It carries money, memories, fear, hope, and history all at once.
People often make rushed choices with houses because they feel cornered, ashamed, sentimental, or pressured.
You will make decisions with clarity, not panic.

This chapter provides you with the practical steps to protect your emotional and financial well-being when a jointly owned home is part of the divorce.

1. Slow down the decision
The biggest mistake people make is believing they must decide immediately whether to sell, stay, or buy the other person out.
You do not.

Divorce courts expect people to take time to sort it out.
Real estate does not move as fast as your emotions.
You are allowed to think.

2. Get the true market value
Never rely on guesswork, Zillow, or what your spouse claims the home is worth.

Get:

a professional appraisal
a comparative market analysis from a realtor
recent sale data in your neighborhood

You cannot negotiate fairly without real numbers.

3. Gather the financial details
Before you can choose anything, you need to know:

your mortgage balance
your monthly payment
your interest rate
your property taxes
your home insurance
your equity
any liens on the home
whether you refinanced during the marriage

Create a folder and place all the documents inside it.
Your future self will thank you.

4. Understand the three real options
All home decisions in divorce fall into one of these paths:

Option A: One spouse keeps the home
Option B: The home is sold and the profit is split
Option C: One spouse buys out the other with cash or assets

Each option has benefits and risks.
Understanding them helps you avoid making emotional choices that can hurt you later.

5. If one spouse keeps the home
This is common, especially if children are involved.

Here is what must happen:

the mortgage must be refinanced into one person's name
the other spouse must be released from liability
the person staying must prove they can afford it
equity must be split or credited as part of the settlement

Do not agree to "I'll keep paying the mortgage, don't worry." If your name is on the loan, lenders hold you responsible. Forever.

6. If the home is sold
Selling brings clarity.

You divide the profits.
You eliminate shared debt.
You both get a fresh start.

If you choose this, agree on:

a realtor
a timeline
repairs or updates
how to handle offers
who lives in the home during the process

Put everything in writing.

7. If a buyout happens
A buyout can be done:

with cash
with other assets

with retirement accounts
with a reduced share of something else

This requires a formal valuation.
Do not allow anyone to guess at the number.

8. Protect yourself from emotional traps
People get attached to their homes for reasons that have nothing to do with logic.

memories
fear of moving
fear of losing status
worry about kids
worry about pets
feeling like "losing the house means losing the marriage"

Remember this truth:
A house is not a life.
It is a building.
Your life moves with you.

9. If children are involved
Courts focus on stability, not houses.
You do not need to keep the home to be a good parent.

Judges look at:

school location
bedroom space
safety

routines
financial stability

Focus on what supports your children in the long run, not what looks good in the short run.

10. Document who pays what during the process
Until things are finalized, keep strict records of:

mortgage payments
repairs
utilities
insurance
HOA dues

If you pay more, you may be reimbursed later.
Documentation keeps things fair.

11. Protect the home physically
If the home is still shared:

secure valuables
record the current condition
photograph each room
remove anything irreplaceable
keep receipts for repairs

This protects you from accusations or misunderstandings.

12. Use ChatGPT to stay organized
Your bot can help you keep track of:

documents
deadlines
mortgage details
emails to your lawyer
conversations with your spouse
task reminders

When emotions run high, organization is your superpower.

13. Do not leave your name on a mortgage you do not control
This is the most common and potentially devastating financial mistake people make.
If your name is on the mortgage, lenders treat you as the responsible party even if:

you moved out
your spouse promised to pay
a temporary agreement was made
your spouse "understands"

If they miss payments, your credit history will be damaged for years.
Do not leave yourself exposed.

14. Think beyond the first year
Divorce makes people think short-term.

Can I afford the mortgage this month?
Can I keep the house for the kids?
Can I survive this transition?

Instead, ask:

Will this house limit my future?
Will it keep me from saving?
Will it trap me in a job I hate?
Will it stop me from rebuilding?

Your next life deserves freedom, not financial chains.

15. It is not a failure if you do not keep the home
Many people feel shame when they sell or move.
Let that go.

Selling can be a smart, strong, strategic decision.
A new home can be peaceful, affordable, and free from emotional weight.

You are not losing your life.
You are redesigning it.

Chapter Twenty-Four

Children, Custody, and Parenting Plans

Nothing in a divorce creates more fear, pressure, or emotion than the future of your children.
Even the calmest people can become terrified versions of themselves when they imagine losing time with their children.

This chapter exists to steady you.
To give you clarity.
To remind you that a parenting plan is not a punishment, a power move, or a measure of love.
It is a structure that supports your children through a major life change.

You and your children deserve a thoughtful, balanced approach.
Let's build it.

---

1. Release the fear that you are "losing" your children

Divorce changes schedules, not love.
You are still their parent.
They still need you.
They still benefit from your presence, even if the weekly rhythm shifts.

Most custody decisions are not about removing a parent.
They are about organizing life.

---

2. Understand the language

Courts use specific terms.
Knowing them reduces anxiety and makes conversations easier:

Legal custody
Who makes major decisions about education, medical care, religion, and overall welfare.

Physical custody
Where the children live and how time is divided.

Joint custody
Both parents share responsibility.

Sole custody
One parent has primary responsibility while the other may have visitation or parenting time.

Parenting time
The schedule of when each parent has the children.

This vocabulary clarifies the process, removing the mystery.

---

3. Courts prioritize one thing

The best interest of the child.

This includes:

stability
school continuity
parental involvement
safety

routines
emotional health
parenting history
each parent's capacity
the child's age and needs

The court is not interested in punishing anyone.
It wants your children to thrive.

---

4. You do not need to be perfect

Many parents spiral into self-blame, worrying that:

they work too much
they don't cook enough
their house is smaller
their job is demanding
their ex has more money

Judges see real families, not Pinterest families.
They do not award custody based on who has the newest car or the fanciest house.

They look for consistency, care, involvement, and emotional safety.

---

5. Start thinking in terms of weekly rhythm, not "winning"

A strong parenting plan answers:

Where do the children sleep during the week?
How do school drop-offs work?
What happens on weekends?
Who handles sports, activities, and appointments?
What about holidays and summer?

Your goal is a plan that reduces friction.
Your children notice stress more than anything else.

---

6. Keep communication professional

During this stage, protect your peace by setting clear communication rules:

everything in writing
no late-night texts
no sarcasm
no threats
no long emotional paragraphs
no putting kids in the middle
no using kids as messengers

Short, calm messages prevent escalation.

If you struggle, let ChatGPT help rewrite your communication in a neutral tone.

---

7. Understand the default schedules courts often use

Most co-parenting plans fall into a pattern such as:

Week-on / week-off
Alternating full weeks

2-2-3 schedule
Two days with one parent
Two days with the other
Alternating three-day weekends

Every-other-weekend plus one weekday
Common when one parent has a demanding schedule

These are starting points, not mandates.

---

8. If your co-parent is difficult

Some parents use children as leverage.
Some stir conflict.
Some refuse to compromise.

Your strength is strategy, not reaction.

Document everything:

missed pick-ups
hostile messages
schedule changes
late payments
efforts you made to cooperate

Documentation protects you.

---

9. Do not bad-mouth the other parent

Even if they deserve it, your children do not benefit from hearing it.

Say instead:

"You have two parents who love you."
"We're figuring things out."
"You don't have to pick sides."
"You're allowed to love both of us."

You set the emotional tone.
Your kids follow your lead.

---

10. Build a parenting plan that fits your real life

Your plan should reflect daily reality, not fantasy.

Ask yourself:

Can I manage school mornings?
Do I have childcare support?
Can I handle after-school chaos alone?
What is best for the kids long-term?

A good plan is sustainable for both parents, even during stressful seasons.

---

11. Negotiate from your children's needs, not your fear

Fear says:

"I need to win this."
"I can't let them have more time."
"If I give an inch, I lose everything."

Clarity says:

"What pattern gives our kids the most stability?"
"What schedule lets both of us show up well?"
"What reduces tension?"

Your children feel the difference.

---

12. Use ChatGPT to prepare

Your bot can help you:

draft proposals
write messages to your lawyer
create sample schedules
prepare scripts for difficult conversations
translate emotional thoughts into calm language
organize your evidence and documents

This is one of the most powerful parts of Divorce Bot.

---

13. Expect guilt, grief, anger, and sadness

These emotions do not mean you are failing.
They mean you love your children.

Divorce reorganizes your family.
It does not erase it.

---

14. Stay steady, even when your ex does not

Your children read your energy.
Your steadiness helps them feel safe.

When your ex escalates, you stay calm.
When your ex lashes out, you respond simply.
When your ex tries to provoke you, you refuse the invitation.

This is strength.

---

15. Your children will be ok because you are showing up for them

The parenting plan is not the end of your story.
It is the beginning of a new one.

You are still their home.
You are still their anchor.
You are still their safe place.

And you are building a life where they can see resilience in action.

Chapter Twenty-Five

Communication Rules During Divorce

Divorce changes every conversation.
Words that once felt simple begin to carry weight. Ordinary questions feel loaded. Neutral statements get misread. Text messages become screenshots. Tone becomes evidence. Silence becomes strategy.

If you want a smoother, safer, and less expensive divorce, you must change how you communicate. Not someday. **Now.**

This chapter gives you clear rules that protect your peace, your finances, and your future.

---

1. Keep Everything Brief, Blunt, and Boring

Your goal is not warmth.
Your goal is not connection.
Your goal is **clarity without emotion**.

A useful test:
Would a judge read this message and think you're calm, steady, and reasonable?

If not, rewrite it.

Examples

- "I will pick up the kids at 6."
- "Can we finalize the repair bill by Friday?"
- "Please send the documents before noon."

Short. Neutral. No color. No commentary.

---

2. Never Argue by Text

Text messages are dangerous. They are fast, emotional, and permanent.

Use text only for logistics.
Never for conflict.
Never for decisions.
Never for emotional topics.

If your ex tries to pull you into a fight by text, respond with:

"I will discuss this at a scheduled time. Not by text."

Then stop.

---

3. Assume Everything Will Be Read by Someone Else

A judge
A lawyer
A mediator
Your ex's new partner
Your own children someday

This rule saves people more money and more dignity than anything else.

Write everything as if it will be held up in court.

If the message makes you cringe, delete it.

---

4. Do Not Explain Yourself

Explaining is emotional labor.
It invites argument.
It gives the other person openings to twist your words.

You do not owe reasons.
You owe **decisions, schedules, and boundaries**.

---

5. Use the "Two-Sentence Rule"

If you cannot say it in two sentences, schedule a call or ask for email.

Two sentences force you to slow down and remove emotion.

---

6. Use Email for Anything Important

Email creates a clean record.
It slows the pace.
It encourages professionalism.
It is easier to keep organized.

This is where you should handle:

- Money
- Custody details
- Scheduling changes
- Agreements
- Anything involving lawyers or mediators

---

7. Do Not Reply Immediately

Silence is not a threat.
Silence is **control**.

Give yourself time to think.
Reread before sending.
Sleep on anything emotional.

Respond only when you are calm enough to act like the person you want to become.

---

8. Remove All Emotion Words

Erase: upset, disappointed, hurt, angry, shocked, frustrated.

Replace with: "I prefer," "I need," "I am requesting," "I will."

Emotion words cost people thousands.
Neutral words save them thousands.

---

9. Never Apologize for Setting a Boundary

A boundary is not rude.
A boundary is protection.

You do not need to soften it.
You do not need to over-explain it.

"I will not discuss that topic."
"I am ending this conversation now."
"We will follow the schedule as written."

Clear. Simple. Done.

---

10. Keep Screenshots, But Don't Announce That You Are Keeping Screenshots

You do not need to give warnings.
You do not need to threaten.

Just document quietly and consistently.

Screenshots help you prove patterns:

- harassment
- pressure
- manipulation
- last-minute schedule changes
- financial inconsistencies

Your lawyer needs facts, not fights.

---

11. Do Not Communicate When You're Exhausted

Late-night conversations create disasters.
Avoid discussing anything after 7 pm.
Your brain needs calm to make good decisions.

Turn off notifications if you must.

This is self-protection.

---

12. Use Divorce Bot for Scripts and Rewrites

Never send a raw emotional message.
Let Divorce Bot rewrite it with these goals:

- Neutral tone
- Clear request
- No emotional hooks
- No invitations to fight

If your ex escalates, Divorce Bot can also generate:

- boundary scripts
- non-engagement responses
- polite refusals
- de-escalation messages
- documentation summaries for your lawyer

You do not have to do this alone.

---

13. Communicate Only When Necessary

You are separating your life. That includes your rhythms, your attention, and your emotional bandwidth.

You do not need to respond to:

- provocation
- guilt

- blame
- insults
- attempts to pull you back into old patterns

You do need to respond to:

- children
- money
- legal matters
- logistics
- emergencies

Everything else can wait or be ignored.

---

14. Stay Consistent

Consistency builds a record that shows:

You are organized.
You are stable.
You are respectful.
You are making decisions in good faith.

Judges respect consistency.

---

15. Speak As the Future You, Not the Past You

The past you was emotional, reactive, exhausted, overwhelmed.
The future you is steady and strategic.

Write messages as if your future self is the one typing them.

You will be amazed at how fast your life improves when you communicate like the person you want to be next.

Chapter Twenty-Six

How To Avoid the Most Expensive Mistakes**

Most divorces don't become financially devastating because of lawyers or court dates.
They become devastating because of **avoidable mistakes** made in moments of fear, anger, or confusion.

This chapter is your shield.
These are the mistakes that drain savings, extend the timeline, and turn a manageable separation into a financial emergency. If you avoid even half of them, you will save thousands of dollars and months of stress.

---

1. Talking Before You Think

The biggest financial mistake is reacting emotionally.
Words spoken in anger can:

- trigger legal action
- damage your credibility
- escalate a peaceful process
- create documentation that can be used against you

If your ex pushes your buttons, pause.
Say nothing until you've cooled down.

A calm message is always more effective than a heated one.

---

2. Hiring the Wrong Lawyer

People choose lawyers based on:

- fear
- pressure
- convenience
- "my friend used them"

Huge mistake.

A great divorce lawyer:

- communicates clearly
- keeps you out of court
- protects your money
- does not escalate conflict
- gives strategy, not drama

A bad lawyer:

- starts fights
- files unnecessary motions
- bills endlessly
- talks for you instead of preparing you
- doesn't explain the process

Interview at least three.
You are hiring them, not the other way around.

---

3. Not Understanding Your Money

Another costly mistake: not knowing your numbers.

You must understand:

- your income
- your spouse's income
- joint and individual accounts
- credit card balances
- loans
- retirement accounts
- insurance policies
- monthly bills
- personal and shared debts

If you don't know your financial picture, someone else will define it for you. And it may not be accurate or fair.

Divorce Bot can help create:

- a financial snapshot
- questions to ask
- a checklist of documents to gather

Knowledge saves money every single time.

---

4. Making Promises Too Early

Never say:

- "You can keep the house"
- "I don't want any money"
- "You can have the car"
- "I just want to be done"

People say these things out of exhaustion.
Then they regret it for years.

Do not give away assets before understanding their long-term value.

---

5. Moving Out Without a Plan

Some people think leaving the house "looks good" or "reduces tension."
Sometimes it does.
Sometimes it destroys your negotiating position.

Before moving out, ask:

- Does this affect custody?
- Does this affect financial claims?
- Does this weaken my stability?
- Will I be expected to continue paying for everything?

Do nothing impulsively.
Do nothing without knowing the legal impact.

---

6. Ignoring Taxes

Divorce shifts tax burdens.
People forget that:

- alimony affects taxes
- who claims the children matters
- selling a house triggers capital gains
- transferring assets may have tax consequences

A fifteen-minute conversation with a tax professional saves thousands.

---

7. Letting Your Ex Control the Narrative

Your ex may try to:

- guilt you
- confuse you
- pressure you
- overwhelm you
- set false timelines

Remember this truth:

Just because they are loud
does not mean they are right
or in control.

Your decisions must be based on facts, not emotion.

---

8. Mixing Dating With Divorce

Dating during a divorce can:

- inflame conflict
- affect custody discussions
- be used against you in court
- create unnecessary emotional strain

You don't need to live like a monk, but stay private, cautious, and calm.

This is a transition period, not a relaunch.

---

9. Hiding Money or Information

People panic and hide assets.
It always backfires.

Courts punish dishonesty more harshly than any financial mistake.
Be transparent.
Be organized.
Be calm.

---

10. Fighting Out of Principle Instead of Strategy

You do not need to win.
You need to land safely.

Battles over:

- furniture
- small assets
- revenge
- "fairness"
- emotional history

cost money you will never get back.

Ask this question before every fight:

"Will this matter five years from now?"

If the answer is no, let it go.

---

11. Letting Fear Make Your Decisions

Fear causes:

- rushing
- agreeing too quickly
- panicking about the future
- overestimating your ex's power
- underestimating your own ability to rebuild

Fear is the most expensive emotion in divorce.

Your job is to slow down long enough to think clearly.
Divorce Bot will help you do exactly that.

---

12. Not Documenting Anything

If it isn't documented, it didn't happen.

Keep:

- receipts
- screenshots
- bank statements
- schedules
- missed pickups
- changes in behavior

- agreements
- conflicts

Documentation wins cases and speeds agreements.

---

13. Trying to Do Everything Yourself

People try to "save money" by not hiring experts.
This usually costs more.

Think strategically:

- a lawyer protects you
- a mediator resolves conflict
- a financial planner saves your future
- Divorce Bot keeps you organized

Delegation is not weakness.
It is wisdom.

---

14. Forgetting to Protect Your Digital Life

Your digital world contains:

- passwords
- banking
- emails
- messages
- cloud storage

- shared subscriptions
- linked devices

One small mistake can expose your information.

You must update everything.
You must separate accounts.
You must protect your privacy immediately.

(We cover this in-depth in later chapters.)

---

15. Believing the Divorce Will End Quickly

It never ends as fast as you think.
Prepare emotionally and financially for a process, not a moment.

That preparation will keep you steady.

Chapter Twenty-Seven

Your Digital Life and Privacy

When a marriage ends, the emotional separation is only half the story. The other half lives in your **phone, cloud storage, passwords, shared logins, financial apps, photos, emails, and every digital footprint the two of you built together.**

If you ignore your digital life, you leave open doors everywhere.
If you protect it, you regain control instantly.

This is one of the most important chapters in the entire book.
Most people don't realize how exposed they are until it is too late.

---

1. Change Every Password Immediately

Do not wait.
Do not assume they won't look.
Do not assume they "aren't that type of person."

People behave unpredictably during divorce.

Update passwords for:

- email
- bank and credit accounts
- Amazon
- Apple ID / Google account
- social media
- cloud services (iCloud, Google Drive, Dropbox)

- utility accounts
- phone carrier
- insurance portals
- health accounts
- retirement logins
- PayPal, Venmo, Cash App
- shared streaming services
- photo storage accounts

Create **strong, unique passwords** and save them in a password manager.

---

2. Turn On Two-Factor Authentication

This is your second lock on the door.

Use authentication apps instead of text messages when possible.
Auth apps are harder to hack and cannot be redirected.

---

3. Remove Their Devices From Your Accounts

Modern tech keeps hidden connections:

- shared iPads
- shared laptops
- smart TVs
- AirTags
- smart speakers
- old phones still logged in

- shared Apple IDs
- shared Google calendars

Go into your settings and remove ANY device that is not yours.

Most people skip this step and regret it.

---

4. Secure Your Phone

Your phone is a vault containing:

- photos
- messages
- documents
- passwords
- contacts
- calendars
- apps that auto-login
- financial tools
- private notes

Protect it by:

- turning off biometric unlocking if they can unlock with your face while you sleep
- enabling a strong passcode
- turning off shared photo albums
- reviewing app permissions
- checking location-sharing settings
- stopping "Find My" sharing

- disconnecting shared Bluetooth devices
- backing up photos and removing personal ones from shared accounts

---

5. Stop Sharing Location

This is critical.

Location sharing can allow an ex to:

- monitor your movements
- show up unexpectedly
- intimidate you
- track spending (by where you go)
- create false narratives

Turn it off without announcement.
You do not need permission to protect your safety.

---

6. Audit Your Email

Your email is the key to everything.
If someone has access to it, they can reset every password you have.

Check:

- forwarding rules
- filters
- auto-deletes
- linked inboxes

- recovery emails
- recovery phone numbers

Ensure nothing routes to your ex.

---

7. Create a Fresh Email for the Divorce

Use a neutral, boring email for:

- your lawyer
- financial advisors
- bank documents
- any private matters

This keeps legal communication away from your old digital patterns.

Example:
yourfirstname.personal2025@email.com

---

8. Separate Your Digital Banking

Joint accounts create opportunities for:

- monitoring your spending
- draining money
- tracking your movements
- altering transaction histories

Open your **own** account now.
Use your new email and phone number.

9. Protect Your Social Media

Your ex (or their friends) may watch your posts.

Do not:

- post about the divorce
- post new dating activity
- post emotional rants
- post anything about money
- post screenshots
- post inspirational quotes aimed at them
- post trips or purchases that look expensive

You are building a legal record of calm stability.

Set everything to private.
Block if necessary.
And post less, not more.

10. Stop Sharing Cloud Storage

Shared cloud accounts contain:

- old tax files
- loan documents
- photos
- private notes
- receipts

• medical details
• kids' info

Move your files to a **new private cloud** and stop syncing old devices.

---

11. Turn Off Shared Calendars

Your ex doesn't need to know:

• your appointments
• meetings
• doctor visits
• lawyer consultations
• trips
• therapy sessions

Clean out all shared calendars or create fresh ones.

---

12. Review Smart Home Devices

If you have:

• Ring doorbells
• Nest cameras
• smart thermostats
• smart locks
• alarm systems
• garage apps

your ex may still have access.

Change every login.
Remove every user.
Reset devices to factory settings if needed.

This protects your physical safety and your peace.

---

13. Lock Down Your Digital Documents

Store important docs in a private, protected folder:

- your ID
- your Social Security card
- your birth certificate
- marriage certificate
- financial documents
- insurance policies
- legal paperwork
- mortgage or lease
- tax returns

This ensures fast access during the divorce.

---

14. Use Divorce Bot for Digital Scripts and Checklists

Tell Divorce Bot:

- "Help me audit my digital security."
- "Rewrite this message to set a boundary about privacy."
- "Walk me through protecting my devices."

- "Help me detach our shared accounts."
- "Create a list of every digital risk I may have missed."

This keeps your digital life clean and safe.

---

15. Privacy Is Power

Once you secure your digital world, you will feel an immediate shift.
You breathe easier.
You think more clearly.
You stop reacting and start leading.

Privacy is not secrecy.
Privacy is safety.

Chapter Twenty-Eight

When You're Being Manipulated

No one enters a marriage expecting to be manipulated.
It starts quietly. It builds slowly.
And during divorce, it often intensifies because control is slipping away.

This chapter is designed to help you recognize manipulation clearly, respond strategically and protect your emotional and financial well-being. You are not here to be intimidated. You are here to stay steady.

---

1. The Shift You Need to Recognize

People often become their most unpredictable when they realize:

- they are losing control
- they are losing access to your time or attention
- they are losing financial stability
- their public image may change
- they can no longer shape your decisions

Manipulation is not always loud.
Sometimes it is quiet, subtle and wrapped in familiar language.

Divorce Bot helps by naming the patterns so you stop doubting yourself.

---

2. Emotional Manipulation

These tactics aim to pull you back into confusion:

• "We don't need lawyers. Let's just handle this ourselves."
• "If you loved me, you wouldn't do this."
• "You're ruining everything."
• "Think about what people will think."
• Sudden apologies that lead nowhere
• Love-bombing after months of withdrawal
• Acting helpless so you fix everything

If someone only becomes kind when they fear losing you, that is not kindness.
That is strategy.

---

3. Financial Manipulation

This is common and powerful:

• hiding money
• delaying payments
• refusing to pay bills
• threatening to cut you off
• offering "agreements" that only benefit them
• pushing you to sign things quickly
• guilt-tripping you over attorney fees
• claiming poverty while spending freely

If money becomes a weapon, take note.
Document everything.
Let numbers speak louder than their words.

---

4. Legal Manipulation

Some people threaten:

- lawsuits
- custody battles
- reporting you for things that never happened
- "taking everything"
- dragging the process out
- making false claims to gain leverage

Threats are not facts.
Threats are meant to destabilize you so you agree to less.

A calm lawyer can dismantle every exaggerated claim.

---

5. Manipulation Through the Children

This is especially painful:

- using kids as messengers
- painting you as the villain
- bribing children to choose sides
- guilt-tripping you for needing time alone
- creating drama during exchanges
- telling the kids details they should never hear

Healthy parents protect children.
Manipulative parents weaponize them.

You stay steady for the kids even when the other person doesn't.

---

6. Manipulation Through Friends and Family

Some people will:

- gather allies
- reshape the narrative
- use mutual friends to pass messages
- pretend to be the victim
- try to isolate you socially
- misrepresent facts to gain sympathy

You don't have to correct anyone.
Silence is often your strongest strategy.

The truth has a long lifespan.
Drama burns out quickly.

---

7. Manipulation Through Guilt

The classic tools:

- "After everything I've done for you…"
- "You're giving up too quickly."
- "You owe me."
- "You're being dramatic."
- "You're making a mistake and you'll regret it."

Let guilt roll off you.
You're choosing stability, not chaos.

---

8. Manipulation Through Confusion

This is deliberate:

• rewriting history
• denying conversations that happened
• flip-flopping endlessly
• overwhelming you with new demands
• sending mixed signals
• pretending not to understand simple requests

Confusion is a control tactic.
Clarity breaks the spell.

Divorce Bot can rewrite messages so they stay clean, calm and direct.

---

9. Manipulation Through Timing

They reach out when you are:

• tired
• stressed
• busy
• sad
• in the car
• with the kids
• at work
• vulnerable
• trying to rest

Chaos becomes their advantage.
Your advantage is choosing **when** to respond.

(You do not owe instant access. Ever.)

---

10. Manipulation Through Sympathy

Watch for the sudden shift:

- tears
- regret
- claims of helplessness
- last-minute crises
- dramatic emotional breakdowns
- "I can't live without you"
- "You're the only one who understands me"

If this behavior only appears when separation becomes real, it is not emotional depth.
It is dependency disguised as love.

---

11. Manipulation Through Fear

Fear is the strongest lever:

- "You'll end up alone."
- "No one will believe you."
- "You can't afford this."

• "You won't survive without me."
• "I'll make your life miserable."

Fear collapses your confidence.
Information restores it.

This book, plus Divorce Bot, keep your footing steady.

---

12. How to Respond

The formula:

1. Stay calm.
2. Respond slowly.
3. Give short answers.
4. Do not explain more than necessary.
5. Stick to facts.
6. Document everything.
7. Avoid texting when emotional.
8. Never negotiate under pressure.
9. Let professionals handle legal decisions.
10. Let time clarify what emotion distorts.

You won't win a power struggle.
You will win by staying outside of it.

---

13. What Manipulation Really Means

It does not mean you are weak.
It does not mean you are foolish.
It does not mean you are dramatic.
It means someone has learned what buttons to push.

Your job is to move the buttons.

---

14. When to Ask for Outside Help

If you feel:

- scared
- overwhelmed
- unstable
- unsure
- trapped
- intimidated
- pressured
- unsafe
- exhausted by the dynamic

reach out to:

- your lawyer
- a therapist
- a trusted friend
- a support group
- a mediator if appropriate

You deserve backup.
No one gets through divorce alone.

---

15. The Power Shift

Once you name manipulation clearly, the spell breaks.

You stop reacting.
You stop hoping they will change.
You stop absorbing the chaos.
You start choosing your steps carefully.
You start building your own life.
You start protecting your energy.
You start feeling like yourself again.

That's the beginning of your freedom.

Chapter Twenty-Nine

Staying Strong During the Process

Divorce is not a single event.
It is a season.
On some days, you'll feel powerful and steady.
Other days you'll feel shaken, tired or worn down.

This chapter provides simple practices to maintain your strength while the legal and emotional waves continue to come.

1. Have a morning anchor

You need one predictable thing every morning that's just for you.

It could be:
- a quiet cup of coffee
- a short walk
- a single page of journaling
- a shower with the bathroom door locked
- five minutes of deep breathing

You are building steadiness, not perfection.

2. Keep your circle small

During a divorce, too many opinions become noise.
Choose only a few trusted people who can:
- listen without adding drama
- support without telling you what to do
- remind you that you're not alone

Quality matters more than quantity.

3. Protect your energy

You do not owe anyone emotional access.
Not your ex.
Not their family.
Not friends who want gossip.

Decide who gets your time and who doesn't.

4. Eat enough, sleep enough

This sounds simple, but it's foundational.
Stress eats energy fast.
Your body needs fuel.

Aim for:
- hydration
- protein
- rest whenever possible
- movement of any kind

Strength starts in the body.

5. Do one thing each day that moves you forward

Just one.

It could be:
- organizing a document
- scheduling a call

- reading a chapter
- taking a break from thinking about divorce entirely

Forward motion—even tiny steps—keeps your confidence alive.

6. Use Divorce Bot for emotional clarity

When you feel overwhelmed, type it all out.
Let Divorce Bot reorganize it into clarity.
You don't have to hold everything in your head anymore.

7. Don't personalize your ex's behavior

Their reactions aren't about who you are.
They're about what they're losing, what they fear and how they cope.

You stay stable by remembering:
"You do you. I'll do me."

8. Know that you are allowed to have good days

Many people feel guilty when they laugh or relax during a divorce.
You're not betraying anything.
You're healing.

9. Watch out for loneliness traps

Loneliness makes you:
- text when you shouldn't
- answer calls you regret
- agree to things you don't want
- question your strength

When loneliness hits, step away from your phone first.
Let the moment pass before making contact.

10. Remind yourself of the future

This chapter isn't about surviving the next hour.
It's about remembering that life after divorce can be full of ease, joy and peace.

Your future is larger than the moment you're in.

Chapter Thirty

When It Finally Ends

There is a moment - a strange, quiet moment — when the papers are signed, the decisions are final and the long stretch of uncertainty comes to a close.
It doesn't arrive with fireworks.
It doesn't feel like a movie ending.
It feels like an exhale you didn't know you'd been holding.

This is what the end really looks like.

---

1. Relief and Disorientation Live Side by Side

When the judge says the words or the final email arrives, you may expect triumph or collapse.
Instead, what you feel is… stillness.

You look around and realize:
This chapter is over.

You don't have to fight anymore.
You don't have to explain anymore.
You don't have to prepare for the next emotional ambush.

But the stillness can feel unfamiliar.
You've spent so long surviving the process that calm feels like a new language.

Let it settle.
You will learn to speak it.

---

2. You May Grieve What Never Happened

People assume grief only comes when you lose something you loved.
But divorce often brings grief for the things you *wanted* but never received:

- the life you pictured
- the partnership you needed
- the version of them you hoped would be
- the version of you that stayed smaller to keep the peace

This grief is real.
It means your expectations were meaningful — and your clarity now is even more meaningful.

---

3. You Also Feel Strength Rising Slowly

The end gives you space to notice what survived:

- your resilience
- your intuition
- your self-respect
- your ability to stand up for your future
- your courage to tell the truth about your life

You didn't break.
You adapted.
And now you get to build.

---

4. The Quiet Practical Steps

After the divorce is final, you do small, steady things:

- update accounts
- revise beneficiaries
- return documents
- close old financial ties
- shift your routines
- reclaim your physical space

These tasks are practical, but they also anchor the new reality:
Your life is your own again.

---

5. The Emotional Echoes Fade

First, you may still:

- think of them during routine moments
- brace for conflict that no longer exists
- feel old habits tug at you
- sense emotional muscle memory

This is normal.
It is not a sign that you made the wrong choice.
It is simply the mind releasing a long-held pattern.

As the weeks pass, the echoes fade.
Your peace becomes louder.

---

6. Your Future Opens Without Permission

You don't need anyone's approval anymore.

You decide:

- how you spend your time
- what your home feels like
- where you go
- who you talk to
- what hobbies you rediscover
- what dreams return
- what boundaries stay firm

This is the quiet beginning of freedom.

---

7. You Become More Yourself Than Before

Divorce does not define you.
But it does refine you.

You learn:

- what you tolerate
- what you need
- what you value
- what you won't compromise again
- how strong you really are

You come back to yourself - not the version that survived the marriage, but the one that rises after it.

This is who you become next.

Chapter Thirty-One

How To Rebuild Your Life

When the divorce ends, rebuilding does not start with a dramatic makeover or a sudden reinvention.
Rebuilding begins quietly, with small choices that steady you and help you return to yourself.
This chapter is about those choices — the ones that create a life that feels safe, honest and fully yours.

---

1. Start With Stability

Before you chase big dreams, give yourself structure.

This can be simple:

- a morning routine that grounds you
- a predictable sleep schedule
- meals that nourish you
- a weekly check-in with yourself
- clean spaces that help your mind rest

Stability is not boring.
It's the foundation that makes every next step stronger.

---

2. Reclaim Your Environment

Your home carries memories of the marriage.
Some stay, some need to go.

Rebuild by reshaping your space:

- remove anything that drags you backward
- add colors, scents and textures that feel like you
- rearrange furniture to reclaim rooms
- replace small things that hold old energy
- introduce new objects that signal a new life

Your home is your anchor now.
Make it reflect who you are becoming.

---

3. Rebuild Your Identity One Layer at a Time

Divorce can leave you asking,
"Who am I without them?"

You discover the answer in layers:

- hobbies you abandoned
- strengths you forgot you had
- confidence you set aside
- dreams you postponed
- passions that waited quietly

This is identity recovery, not reinvention.
You are not creating a new you.
You are letting the original you return.

---

4. Strengthen Your Financial Footing

Money is part of rebuilding.
It gives you choice and control.

Do these early:

- set a new personal budget
- list every recurring expense
- explore new income options
- automate savings
- check credit reports
- clean up old financial ties

Financial confidence rebuilds emotional confidence.
When you feel safe, everything else becomes possible.

---

5. Rebuild with People Who Support You

You are not meant to rebuild alone.

Choose relationships that:

- listen without judgment
- keep your confidence
- respect your boundaries
- bring encouragement
- remind you of your worth

Let go of anyone who reopens wounds or keeps you stuck in old roles.

Your new circle doesn't need to be big.
It needs to be honest.

---

6. Rediscover Joy Without Apology

Joy might feel strange at first.
Divorce often rewires your emotional system, and joy can feel unfamiliar or undeserved.

Start small:

- a favorite drink
- a walk in the sun
- a new creative project
- a book that pulls you in
- an experience you always wanted to try

Joy is not frivolous.
It is medicine.

---

7. Your New Story Is Not a Reaction to Your Old One

The goal is not to prove anything to your ex or to erase the past.

The goal is to build a life that reflects your truth.

This chapter of your life:

- honors your resilience
- grows from your experience
- focuses on what matters most
- is not shaped by their shadow

You are writing forward now.

---

8. Rebuilding Is Not Linear

You will have moments when you feel strong and clear, followed by moments when emotions return unexpectedly.

This does not mean you're going backward.

It means:

- you are healing
- your mind is processing
- you are adjusting to freedom
- you are learning new rhythms

Rebuilding takes time, but every step counts.

---

9. Look for Signs of Growth

Growth shows up quietly:

- you breathe easier
- you feel lighter in your own home
- you make decisions faster
- you trust your intuition
- you stop explaining yourself
- you start dreaming again

This is what rebuilding looks like.

---

10. You Are Allowed to Build a Life You Love

Divorce doesn't end a story.
It begins a new one.

A story where:

- you choose your path
- you trust your voice
- you protect your peace
- you value your needs
- you live without shrinking
- you take up your full space

This new life belongs to you.

You earned it.
You get to enjoy it.
You get to grow in it.
You get to thrive.

Chapter Thirty-Two

Who You Become Next**

Divorce does not define you.
It reveals you.

When the dust settles, you begin to see the person underneath the roles you have carried for so long.
This chapter is about that moment.
The moment when you look ahead and realize your future is not a reaction to your past.
It is a creation.

---

1. You Become Someone Who Knows Yourself

During marriage, identity often gets blended, muted or stretched to fit someone else's needs.
After divorce, you return to your original self, the one who existed before compromise became habit.

You become a person who:

• knows what you like
• knows what you will not tolerate
• honors your instincts
• trusts your inner voice
• sees your own strength

This is your new baseline.

---

2. You Become Someone Who Sets Boundaries without Apology

Boundaries are not walls.
They are the shape of your peace.

After divorce, you gain the clarity to say:

- no to old patterns
- no to draining relationships
- no to emotional manipulation
- no to guilt that isn't yours

You stop overexplaining.
You stop shrinking your needs.
You stop carrying responsibility that never belonged to you.

This is what growth looks like.

---

3. You Become Someone Who Chooses with Intention

Instead of reacting to frustration or survival, your choices start coming from stability and desire.

You choose:

- work that fits your values
- people who respect your energy
- commitments that leave you room to breathe
- routines that help you thrive

Your life becomes something you build on purpose.

**4. You Become Someone Who Can Love Again

Including Yourself**

Love after divorce is different.
It is slower, wiser, gentler, more honest.

But before you love someone else, you learn to love yourself in new ways:

- the way you survived
- the way you kept going
- the way you protected your heart
- the way you rebuilt what broke

You learn that you deserve love that doesn't wound or diminish you.

When love comes again, it will meet you as the person you have become, not the person you had to be.

---

5. You Become Someone with a Future Again

Divorce can temporarily shrink your world.
But as healing takes hold, your life expands.

You begin to imagine:

- new routines
- new adventures
- new friendships
- new places to live
- new versions of yourself

Your future stops feeling like something you fear and starts feeling like something you shape.

This is when you know you are through the hardest part.

---

6. You Become Someone Who Knows They Can Survive Anything

Once you survive a divorce, you learn a powerful truth:

There is nothing you cannot handle.

Your confidence becomes internal, not situational.
Your stability comes from within, not from someone else's presence.
Your strength is no longer theoretical.
It is lived, proven and earned.

This chapter is about that identity.
The one waiting patiently for you on the other side.

You become someone new.
You become someone true.
You become someone whole.

****Bonus Section**

DivorceBot Tools**

This is the toolbox section designed to help readers take action, stay organized and reduce stress.
These pages give structure, clarity and momentum — exactly what people

need when life is upside down.
Each tool is simple, direct and easy to use.

Tool 1: Scripts for Difficult Conversations

Divorce requires communication during moments when communication feels impossible.
These short scripts help you get through conversations without being pulled into conflict.

Telling your spouse you want separation:
"I need time and space to think clearly. I want us to speak through email or text so we can both stay calm and organized."

Responding to hostility:
"I'm willing to discuss this when we can both speak respectfully. I'm stepping away now and will reply when things cool down."

Setting a boundary:
"I will not discuss this topic when it turns into a fight. Let's focus on what needs to be solved, not the past."

Communicating about children:
"Let's keep our conversations centered on the kids and their needs. Personal comments do not help them."

Tool 2: Documentation Checklist

Document everything.
It protects you, clarifies the facts and strengthens your case.

Keep records of:

- texts, emails and voicemails
- financial statements
- account balances
- mortgage documents
- property titles
- insurance policies
- tax returns
- childcare schedules
- agreements made verbally
- copies of all legal filings

Tool 3: Personal Inventory Worksheet

This helps you identify what is yours, what matters most and what you want to protect.

List:

- personal items
- family heirlooms
- tools or equipment you purchased
- professional items
- sentimental possessions
- jewelry
- artwork

- digital assets
- passwords
- subscriptions

Tool 4: Divorce Preparation Checklist

A step-by-step guide for the early weeks.

Week One:

- secure important documents
- open a private email
- begin documenting everything
- change passwords
- speak to a lawyer
- protect your credit

Weeks Two and Three:

- create a budget
- freeze joint spending if permitted
- begin separating accounts
- track childcare schedules
- gather financial statements

Weeks Four and Five:

- meet with mediation or legal teams
- establish boundaries
- reorganize your home
- prepare for temporary agreements

Tool 5: Financial Snapshot Worksheet

A simple overview to help you understand your financial foundation.

Monthly Income:

- salary
- freelance or contract work
- child support
- alimony

Monthly Expenses:

- housing
- insurance
- transportation
- childcare
- food
- debt payments

Assets:

- savings
- retirement accounts
- property
- vehicles
- investments

Liabilities:

- credit cards
- loans
- mortgages

Tool 6: Rebuild-Your-Life Plan

A guided plan to help you regain momentum.

Step One:
Stabilize your living situation.

Step Two:
Create a realistic budget.

Step Three:
Rebuild your social circle.

Step Four:
Set three achievable goals for the next 90 days.

Step Five:
Choose one new habit that supports the life you want.

Tool 7: Resources and Support

A curated list you can fill in or adapt.

- local women's centers
- legal aid offices
- mediation services
- counseling resources
- trauma-informed therapists
- parenting coordinators
- financial planners
- support groups

- community classes
- books and learning materials
- online forums

These resources remind readers they are not alone and support is always available.

Closing Page

Divorce reshapes a life, but it does not diminish it.
If you made it to the end of this book, you already proved something important.
You kept going.
You stayed curious.
You chose to understand rather than collapse.
You reached for tools instead of despair.

That matters.
It means you are already stronger than you realize.

Divorce Bot exists for one reason.
To help you think clearly when everything feels tangled.
To help you stay grounded when emotions run high.
To remind you that your future is still wide open.

Take what helps.
Leave what doesn't.
Use these tools as a stepping stone, not a cage.
Build the next season of your life with intention, with courage, and with the quiet belief that you deserve a life that fits you better than the one you left.

You are not behind.
You are not broken.
You are not alone.

You are becoming.
And this is only the beginning.

About the Author

Sugar Gay Isber McMillan is a Texas artist, designer, educator and author of more than sixty books, including a growing collection on ChatGPT and creative technology. Her work explores how art, history and modern tools shape the way people learn, create and navigate major life changes.

Sugar has designed jewelry for film, television, museums and private collections worldwide. She serves as the Creative Ambassador for Fire Mountain Gems, hosts Jewelry Stars with Sugar Gay Isber on Made It Myself TV and teaches jewelry design at Austin Community College.

She holds a B.A. in Journalism, M.A.s in Humanities and Visual Arts and an advanced degree in Information Technology. Certified in ChatGPT for Business Applications through Microsoft, she also works as a technical writer for a global technology company.

Through The WOW Book Co., Sugar creates books that blend clarity, storytelling and practical guidance for readers of all ages.

About the Talk to Your Tools Series

Talk to Your Tools is Sugar's collection of practical guides that show readers how to use ChatGPT as a thinking partner. Each book helps you think better, feel steadier, create with confidence and bring more clarity to your daily life. The series turns technology into a simple, supportive tool for personal growth.

Follow Sugar

Instagram: @SugarGayIsber
Amazon Author Page: amazon.com/author/sugargayisbermcmillan
Website: TheWOWBookCo.com
For media or collaborations: GayIsber@gmail.com

Made in the USA
Monee, IL
08 November 2026

67950726R20114